LANGUAGE THROUGH LITERATURE

A Pragmatic Approach for Tribal Learners

LANGUAGE THROUGH LITERATURE

A Pragmatic Approach for Tribal Learners

PREETINANDA ROY

AUTHORSPRESS

Worldwide Circulation through Authorspress Global Network
First Published in 2022
by
Authorspress
Q-2A Hauz Khas Enclave, New Delhi-110 016 (India)
Phone: (0) 9818049852
E-mail: authorspressgroup@gmail.com
Website: www.authorspressbooks.com

Language through Literature:
A Pragmatic Approach for Tribal Learners
ISBN 978-93-5529-270-4

Printed in India at Thomson Press (India) Limited

Dedicated to Dr Manmath Kundu, my guide, mentor and supervisor and Dr Binodini Patra for immense love, affection and encouragement in completing this task...

Acknowledgement

This book has been possible by the grace of God, the Almighty, despite my daunting commitment at home and workplace. In conceptualizing, preparing and finalizing the paper, my Supervisor and Guide, Dr Manmmath Kundu, Former Academic Advisor, ELTI, Bhubaneswar, has steered and improved the paper all through, sparing his valuable time and responding to my frequent calls without demur. I owe him a deep debt of gratitude. I am grateful to Madam, Dr BinodiniPatra, Former Reader in English, BJB College, Bhubaneswar, who has been to me a pillar of strength and an unfailing source of strength and guidance.

The book couldn't have been a reality, but for the generosity of Dr AchyutaSamanta, the Hon'ble Founder, KIIT & KISS and Member of Parliament, who accorded me permission to pursue research work, while in regular service. I convey my profound gratitude to him. The Hon'ble Vice Chancellor, KISS Deemed-to be-University, Prof. Deepak Kumar Behera, Registrar and CEO, KISS, Dr Prashanta Kumar Routray have actively supported, inspired and encouraged me to publish this book for which I am deeply indebted to them.

I am grateful to Dr. Sujata Acharya, Principal, KISS for all her cooperation.

I owe indebtedness and profound gratitude to Dr. Chitta Ranjan Bhoi, Associate Professor, KISS Deemed-to be-University, who always motivated and guided me in my academic pursuit and extended all support in making this book a reality.

For collection of data and materials, I am grateful to the Faculty Members of Dept. of English, the Librarian, Kalinga Institute of Social Sciences and above all, students of Kalinga Institute of Social Sciences, for whom this research is aimed at and could be made possible.

I am grateful to Authorspress, New Delhi, for considering my paper for publication and making my dream into a reality.

Last but not the least, I must acknowledge the unwavering support and co-operation of my family members but for whom the paper wouldn't have seen the light of the day. I shall remain ever indebted to them.

Preetinanda Roy (Ph.D)

Preface

India is a land of multi-culturalism and multi-lingualism. The ethnic diversity that our country offers is not found anywhere in the world. The culture has been enriched by the substantial contribution of the tribal and the non-tribal as well. The tribal population of India is about 40 million which comprises of three hundred different tribal communities. They are backward in many respects due to their primitive way of life and their state of relative isolation from the society. Ample provision has been made in the Constitution of India as they have been explicitly identified among the weaker section. Language skill, which forms the basis of every other form of learning, faces complex problems for the tribal due to existence of numerous tribal languages and dialects. The problem gets worsened because many of the tribal communities do not have scripts of their own. Tribal pupils are at a disadvantage as the regional language in which they are taught is often their second or third language. English, which is so very important in the Indian context, becomes their third or fourth language and an extra burden. The need for English in higher education, is obvious. The representation of the tribal in professional courses and in Class 1 government services is very minimal mostly owing to their lack of proficiency in English.

The Constitution of India, Article 366 (25) defines Scheduled Tribes as "such tribes or tribal communities or part of or groups within such tribes or tribal communities as are deemed under Article 342 to the scheduled Tribes (STs) for the purposes of this Constitution". In Article 342, the procedure to be followed for specification of a scheduled tribe is prescribed. The Commission for

Scheduled Castes and Scheduled Tribes in its report has listed some common features of this community.

- They live away from the civilized world mostly in the inaccessible parts lying in the forests and hills.
- They belong to either one of the 3 stocks – Negrito, Austroloids or Mongoloids.
- They speak the tribal dialect.
- They profess primitive religions known as 'Animism' in which the worship of the ghosts and spirits is of utmost importance.
- They follow primitive occupations such as gleaning, hunting and gathering of forest products.
- They are largely carnivorous or meat eaters.
- They have nomadic habits and a love for drink and dance.

But in the present context, most of the above features have lost their relevance and there is no clear indication or criteria for specifying them. But it appears that the following three aspects are taken into consideration:

- Tribal origin
- Primitive way of life
- General backwardness

A person is said to be a Scheduled Tribe if he belongs to any of the tribes specified in the Government list in the present context. The Scheduled Tribe groups who were identified as more isolated from the wider community and who maintain a distinctive cultural identity have been categorised as 'Particularly Vulnerable Tribal Groups' (PTGs) (previously known as Primitive Tribal Groups) by the Government at the Centre.

The state of Odisha has the highest variety of tribes as well as the maximum tribal population. There are 62 tribal communities with a population of 95,90,756, constituting 22.8% of the total population of the state and 13.34% of India's total tribal population (census 2011). They mostlyinhabit the remote parts of the state lacking all basic amenities where they have to face varieties of problems. The root problem in their education is language learning.

The study is based on the proposition that the tribal students are poor in English, and that, this is the major factor responsible for their poor attainment in higher education. A corollary to this is the postulation that English language is difficult for them. The remaining assumptions that contribute to the main hypotheses are their poor socio-economic backgrounds; they are first generation learners with low academic aspirations and low motivation which affect their higher education; they are orthodox and superstitious which obstruct their learning English. Their happy-go-lucky nature is a major demotivating factor for higher education in general and learning English in particular. They have a sense of inferiority among the tribal pupils about their academic achievements and achievement in English. English being their fourth language, they have special linguistic problems in learning English. The school system which reflects middle class values, is foreign to their culture and background and existing English text books create cultural problems for them.

The objective of the book is

1. To investigate the problems of tribal learners in learning English.
2. To evaluate the prescribed materials of English teaching for Higher secondary classes under the Council of Higher Secondary Education, Odisha.
3. To evaluate how effective are the prescribed materials for their learning.
4. To examine that if the tribal learners are taught English through tribal learner's friendly materials and methods, they will learn English better.

The book evaluates the prescribed poems as a whole which included the introduction of the poem and the poet, notes and glossary, understanding the poem, appreciation of the poem, activities undertaken i.e. pre-reading, while-reading, post-reading, questions asked, activities both oral and written. There after the tribal learner friendly poems are shortlisted and experimented with the activities suggested by the author. Observations are made to find out the improvement in learning of the students. These experiments continued till the final objective is achieved.

Chapter I states the problem, the plan, the scope and the methodology of the study. It argues further that most of the studies done earlier are general in nature and confined to socio-economic aspects. Moreover no work has been done to identify the problems of the tribal in learning of English language through poetry.

Chapter-II makes an analysis of the prevailing trends in the study of English literature specifically Poems in teaching language to the "disadvantaged minority learners" in Odisha. The available educational programmes for them are detailed, their need for English is ascertained and the necessary provisions made for the teaching of English is stated.

Chapter-III presents a survey of the English education of tribal in Odisha, particularly in Kalinga Institute of Social Sciences (KISS). It attempts to evaluate the Government measures provided for their English education. It also justifies the need of English learning for mainstreaming and upward mobility of the target community. It argues that the existing system of education has a "detribalizing" effect on them.

Chapter IV deals with the Field work. For example administration of a test of proficiency in English language through learning of poetry, questionnaires to teachers of English as well as students at KISS in Higher Secondary level regarding the proficiency of the tribal learners, their problems, methodologies adopted by them while teaching and the survey of existing stereotypes. Chapter V deals with the suggestions for Material

Preparation for the tribal learners which would be most suitable for them basing on the result of the survey conducted.

Chapter VI depicts the tryouts and experimentations on the suitability of the proposed poems for the tribal learners. This tryout and experimentations are repeated again and again using different suggested methodologies suggested till they achieve a standard level of learning. Findings comes next which explains the outcome of the experimentations and try outs done while teaching poetry to tribal learners using different suggested methodologies in achieving a standard level of learning.

The concluding chapter attempts to arrive at some conclusions and suggestions on instructional strategies .for teaching English poetry to tribal pupils with suggested changes in English Poetry curricula, text-books, methods of teaching, evaluation and teacher training.

The study is limited to teaching of English to tribal learners, more specifically teaching poems in English. Geographically, the scope of the study is limited to Odisha to the globally renowned tribal residential institution Kalinga Institute of Social Sciences (KISS), Bhubaneswar where 30,000 tribal learners are provided with education, food, cloth and all basic needs in one campus free of cost. The scope of the study is further delimited to Higher Secondary level.

Contents

List of Tables

List of Figures

1

Introduction

India is a vast land of incredibility and diversity. The variety that our country offers in people, their costume, language, religion etc. occupies a unique place in the entire world. The only element that links the whole country in unison is the attitude of being Indian and; the link language, Hindi and English. Though English is being taught as a second or foreign language in educational institutions, the importance of English in India can easily be understood as it is accorded the associate official language status. So far higher education and career growth is concerned, it can be said to be the only language which promises to give a leap in career. English is an international language, spoken in many countries as a native or as a second or foreign language. It is the language of communication among countries, the language of trade and commerce, science and technology, medicine and law, global news and views etc. Above all it is the language of library and higher education. So a student in India cannot just do away with this language.

The tribal, also called Scheduled Tribes (ST) or *Adivasis* have low levels of literacy and are most backward community socially, economically and more importantly, educationally. Their lack of proficiency is considered as one of the barriers to their education, apart from the fear of learning a foreign language, which is not at all complementary to their mother tongue. At higher level, English language is a criterion rather than an option. The Article 348 of Indian Constitution has accorded English as one of the official language status besides Hindi. But still, this language is one of the major obstacles for the tribal in their education. The tribal lag behind their non-tribal counterparts in education. The root problem in their education is language education. Tribal people mostly have their own dialects in spoken and written language. Thus, the tribal learners are found to be poor in English language skills.

The population of Odisha has a high concentration as well as the greatest variety of tribes. It has 62 tribal communities and their population constitutes approximately 23% of the total population of the state and 13.34% of India's total tribal population. They are inhabited mostly in the remote parts of the state where there is a lack of all basic amenities which are easily available to the general people. When it comes to education, they have to face varieties of problems. The root problem in their education is language education. They have their own mother tongues which are different from the state language. Education through their mother tongue has so far not been possible and more over their language is considered as minority language in India. Hence, they get educated through state language. In Indian context, learning English is inevitable. Most of the states in India start teaching of English from primary level. Thus the tribal learner's problems in language education get extended to their English language education. They are found to be poor in English language skills.

Teaching language through literature is, of course, a very useful and pragmatically strategy. In fact, the strategy has been a recognized approach in ELT, especially in countries, where English is reckoned as a second or foreign language. As a matter of fact, the approach doesn't help in learning English as the focus is more on literature than learning the language through literature. However, it is an undeniable fact that literature and language are complementary to each other. This is true in most of the current courses of English poems both at college and school level. English is a native language of more than 300 million people and second language of 350 million people worldwide. But, the problems get worsened when the learners have low proficiency in linguistic competence like the tribals in our country. Poems, however, offer a rich, varied repertoire and are a source of much enjoyment to both teachers and learners alike, and it has a great potential for teaching language in a more interesting and effective way. But unfortunately, the potential of poetry has not fully been exploited to teach language.

This study is conducted to understand educational backwardness of tribal learners with special reference to English language. This study intends to reverse the trend profitably by using poems with high pedagogic potential to help learners develop both literary and language skills. In order to reverse the current trend, teachers have to modify their teaching strategies and the materials that should be close to the learners' level and interest. In students' perspective the current courses of poetry do not satisfy their needs and interests. They need courses that meet their needs. They are more concerned with studying language rather than literature. The proposed study tries to meet the students' interests and needs through a selection of learners friendly and need based simple and interesting poems with mind-engaging language activities. This study tries to link language and literature through an anthology of poems for the tribal learners. And it mainly aims at providing the teacher with a set of suitable poems with language activities which can be used even with classes of tribal learners who are struggling to set right their basic English potential and further, they can be encouraged to enjoy poems and develop both their language and literary skills, doing the interesting activities. The Poetry course, thus, becomes more interesting, motivating and an asset and not a liability – something that they have not just to memorize and vomit in the exam, but a real course of EDUTAINMENT.

The present study has been undertaken with two sets of aims – investigating the problems of tribal learners of English and suggesting a viable instructional strategy for teaching them English. The approach is mainly empirical, making use of field research. Although a detailed study of current trends in teaching the "disadvantaged", particularly, learners belonging to the ethnic minorities, and of literatures on the tribals and their culture, gives the study its broad conceptual framework.

1. Teaching poetry is a very important component of teaching literature and literature, moreover forms a very important part of the courses offered by the Council of Higher Secondary Education, Odisha. Unfortunately, teaching poetry to the students, does not achieve the real objective – to teach language through literature to help learners improve their English Language skills. The focus, on the contrary, is more on literature than on learning the language through literature. Current courses of English poems suffer from this flaw. The courses do not serve the need and interest of the students as it is too literary, even old and archaic. The proposed study intends to design material which, it is hoped, will be of a great benefit to both teachers and more particularly to students. Having outlined the approach, now it remains to describe the problem. For the purpose of the study, the problem can be formulated as a set of questionnaire to which answers are sought in the subsequent chapters which are detailed below:
2. What socio-economic problems do the tribal learners face in learning English?
3. Which of these were "unique to them? In which way does their home environment affect their learning?
4. What ethnic and cultural factors obstruct their learning of the language?
5. Do their attitudes to English, the English teacher and English class affect their performance in the subject?
6. What linguistic problem do they have?
7. What is the attitude of English teachers to the tribal learner's academic achievement, his language and culture?

Assumptions were made based on these questions and instruments were designed to verify them. But to put the problem in a broader perspective a global survey of teaching to the "disadvantaged" and ethnic minority is attempted in Chapter II and an objective analysis of the activities of the Government to the education of the tribals in India in Chapter III.

The scope of the study has been delimited by: Selecting one particular state of India, i.e. Odisha for study. Confining the study to a narrower geographic region, Kalinga Institute of Social Sciences (KISS), Bhubaneswar, Odisha Selecting students, teachers, ELT problems at +2 1st year level only. The reasons for confining the study to Odisha are as follows:

The state has a high concentration as well as the greatest variety of tribes. There are 62 tribal communities in Odisha. The tribal population constitutes 23.11% of the total population of the state and 13.34% of India's total tribal population.

English serves important functions in the state.

It plays an important role both in educational system as a medium of communication and in the selection tests for recruitment in different government and non-government positions. A good command over English will therefore, will favour the tribals' opportunities in employments. The researcher being a resident of the state is more familiar with the varied socio-economic-politico and cultural pattern of the tribals. The state also has a very high concentration of tribal population, and thus who are chosen for the present study.

The following reasons can be ascribed in favour of delimiting the study further to KISS – the world famous largest tribal residential institution of Odisha.

The largest tribal residential institute in the world with 30,000 children from KG to PG, getting free education, free boarding and food. It is unquestionably a prototype of a miniature Odisha in true sense with students from all 62 tribes and 13 primitive tribes. The researcher, being closely associated with this institute for last 15 years, has a rich experience and special inclination towards these tribal students and their education. In the present study it has been confined to the first year of Higher Secondary level for the following reasons:

- The teaching of English in Odisha starts from Class IV and the problems of learners are better understood after they have learned English for a few years.
- Tribal students become conscious of their difficulties in learning English when they go to college when they are supposed to set clear goals for their future.
- At this level, their feedback will be of great help to pinpoint their problem which they come across.
- The English course is more uniform at this stage.
- English courses, too, diversify faster and further as education tends to diversify after the school stage,.

The scope of the study is limited to teaching of poems to the tribal learners at the Kalinga Institute of Social Sciences, Bhubaneswar. The study is concerned with 'what' and 'how' of teaching English poetry. Poetry crept into language classroom from time past as teachers realized that poems could be instrumental in developing literary and language skills in the learners. This study shows how poem can also be used effectively to upgrade language skills – through listening (to the teacher while reciting the poem); through speaking (through discussing the poem with the teacher); through reading (over and over the text as a byproduct of doing the interesting activities). And more importantly all these are to be achieved in an interesting and joyful way. The text are to be provided with activities and questions so that the students, in order to answer the questions and do the activities, simultaneously have to go back to the text over and over again; the unconscious by-product of which will be exposure to English through poems.

The basis of the need for the present study is considered to be imperative and justifiable for the following reasons.

- Both the Central and the State Governments are vitally interested in the all-round development of the tribals, and education has been accepted as the main instrument for their upward mobility.

- But, in spite of, all these attempts, reports of the various Commissions on tribals show a wide gap between the expectations and the real achievement. As very few tribal students go in for higher and technical education and their representation in Class I and II jobs seem to be very negligible.
- From the researcher's experience with tribal learners it is understood that the learners have specific problems in learning English and apart from that, their poor command over English is considered to be the main obstacle for persuing technical studies and opportunities to employment as well.
- Though some studies have been conducted on the education of tribal in general, no study is so far conducted to address the learning of English.
- Current course is too literature-oriented.
- The tribal students at KISS, though provided with adequately unique opportunity to mainstream themselves, they do fail to acquire the vital traits in English language skill like development of linguistic skills which alone can enhance their chances of getting through all various top grade services inside and outside the state.
- About 80% of the tribal learners who join college are low-proficient and having no or little basic knowledge in English. So they cannot cope with the much higher standard English at college level. And such difficult poems at college level do not help them in ameliorating their language skills.
- There is an urgent need for shifting from teaching English poetry to developing literary skills with a view to developing both literary and language skills putting emphasis on

language skills. We have long tradition of teaching poems as a part of the course curriculum at the college level.

The study involved extensive field works, the detailed reporting of which is done later. The instruments for field work were designed keeping in view the hypotheses listed above and the investigation was conducted in first year class of Higher Secondary Class in KISS where the strength of first year class is 1440 in all the three streams with approximately 120 students in each section. The field work included the following:

1. A test of proficiency in English, questionnaire to the teachers of tribal pupils, interview,
2. Case studies,
3. Observation of English classes
4. Analysis of text books and tests in English.

To begin with, the study made a survey of teaching poems to help learners learn English. The study showed how English poetry is taught in the first year class of Higher Secondary in KISS. There is also the field survey which is concerned with the evaluation of materials, courses, methods of teaching modules and tests. The survey, part of the study, makes use of such methods of social science research as administration of questionnaire, interviews, evaluation and observation, The main part of the study is about designing materials (an anthology of poems) and trying them out in a group of learners of the third level.

2

Teaching English to Tribal Learners

India has the largest Tribal population in the world. The tribal population of 104.28 million constitutes 8.61% of the total population of India as per 2011 census. According to the Article 342 of the Indian constitution, there are 697 tribes in India and out of those, 62 tribes reside in Odisha alone. Their livelihood is primarily dependent on primitive agriculture, hunting and gathering type, without the use of technology, which is the main cause of their poverty. Besides, they have low level of literacy which is a serious threat to Indian education system. Their social deprivation is reflected in their educational backwardness.

Taking into account such criteria as caste, levels of literacy and economic status, many come under the term "disadvantaged" in India. SCs and STs are among the most disadvantaged socio-economic group of India suffering from extreme social, economical backwardness. Hence, the Scheduled Castes and the Scheduled Tribes have been accorded official "disadvantaged" status. The Article 342 of Constitution of India, specifically identifying STs among the most weaker sections of the society, has made ample provision for their upliftment. In addition to the Preamble, a series of articles provide for their protection and welfare (Constitution of India).

Scheduled Tribes, also referred to as STs, are rightly called the 'Adivasi'. This term justifies their contribution to Indian life and culture. Tribal people have their own unique culture, language and lifestyle. A good rendering of '*Adibasi*' in English would be, perhaps, 'aboriginal.' without the stigma to some extent, attached to the English word. A better equivalent is "Bhumiputra" – sons of the soil – which is used in Indonesia to identify the people native to the country. It was difficult on the part of anthropologists to give the present Scheduled Tribes a common definition. Broadly the term refers to *"territorial communities, the bulk of whom live in relative isolation of hills and forests"* (Sachidanand, 1967: 202). The Commission for Scheduled Castes and Scheduled Tribes in its report for the year 1952 has listed following eight common features of these communities.

- They live away from the civilized world in the inaccessible parts lying in the forests and hills.
- They belong to either one of the 3 stocks such as, Negrito, Austroloid or Mongoloid.
- They speak the same tribal dialect.
- They profess primitive religions known as "Animism" in which, the worship of 'ghosts' and 'spirits' is the most important.
- They follow primitive occupations such as gleaning, hunting and gathering of forest products.
- They are largely carnivorous or meat eaters.
- They live either naked or semi-naked using tree barks or leaves as clothes.
- They have nomadic habits and a love for drink and dance.

But, it seems, most of these features have lost their relevance at present for identifying the Scheduled Tribes.

In the present context, here is no clear indication of the criteria for specifying them. But it appears that the following three such aspects are taken into considerations: tribal origin, primitive way of life, general backwardness.

A person is said to belong to a Scheduled Tribe if he belongs to any of the tribes specified in the Scheduled Tribes and Scheduled Castes List officially specified by the Government. The term, therefore, is meaningful only in the context of legal provisions, Government policies and measures.

> The diverse groups included in the list prefer to identify themselves by their traditional tribe names. It has, therefore, in the present context, few social or cultural implications. It has become the catch word for the political consciousness of a particular group of people in the country, which has become symbolic of privileged treatment (Mathur, 1972: 457-461).

Their tribal origin, language and relatively isolated life differentiate them from the Scheduled Castes. Unlike the Scheduled Tribes, the Scheduled Castes live not in isolated communities but in multi caste villages where they are often residentially segregated and speak the language of the dominant community. Thus, the tribal, in general, display the following characteristics:

- Rigid social order
- Animism
- Alcoholism
- Strong group solidarity
- Existence of taboos
- Belief in the supernatural.

The Scheduled Tribe groups who were identified as more isolated from the wider community and who maintain a distinctive cultural identity have been categorised as 'Particularly Vulnerable Tribal Groups' (PTGs) (previously known as Primitive Tribal Groups) by the Government at the Centre.

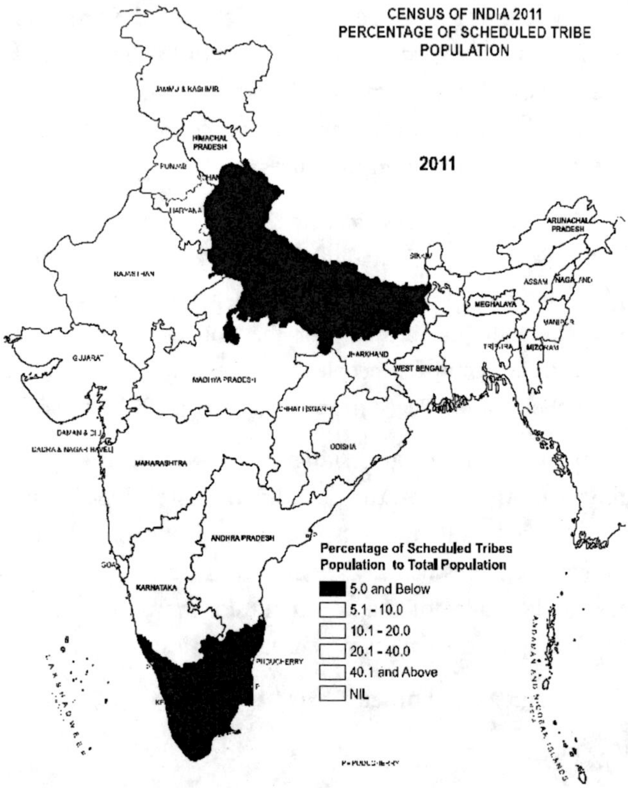

Figure No. 2.1: Census of India 2011 Percentage of Scheduled Tribe Population

The principal aim of the Government is to empower the principal stake holders through their educational, economic and social development in order to build self-reliance and self-esteem among them. The vision and mission of the ST & SC Development and Minorities & Backward Classes Welfare Department is all-round development of the Scheduled Castes, Scheduled Tribes, Other Backward Classes and Minority communities vis-a-vis other sections of the society. Odisha occupies a unique position among the Indian States and Union Territories for having a rich and colourful tribal scenario. Majority of Scheduled Tribes live in hilly and forest regions. Their economy is largely subsistence oriented, non-stratified and non-specialized. Their social system is simple and aspirations and needs are limited. Though the Scheduled Tribes in Odisha have suffered from social, educational and economic backwardness due to geo-historical reasons, they have their own distinctiveness and social-cultural milieu. The process of socio-economic development is going on after independence and has picked up momentum. 62 Scheduled Tribes in Odisha speak as many as 74 dialects. Their ethos, ideology, worldview, value-orientations and cultural heritage are rich and varied. At one end of the scale there are nomadic food gatherers and hunters and at the other end, skilled settled agriculturists and horticulturists. The tribal areas of Odisha, therefore, present an extremely diverse socio-economic panorama.

According to 2011 Census, the tribal population of the State is 95,90,756 constituting 22.85% of the total population of the State and 9.66% of the total tribal population of the country. There are 62 different tribal communities including 13 Particularly Vulnerable Tribal Groups (PVTGs) in the State. Odisha has the third largest concentration of tribal population in the country. About 44.70% of the State's geographical area which is known as Scheduled Area, extends over 118 out of 314 Blocks in 12 districts and a portion of Suruda Tahsil of Ganjam District. The Scheduled Tribe population of Scheduled Area accounts for about 68.09% of total tribal population of the State. The remaining tribal population inhabit in MADA / Cluster pockets and are dispersed in other areas that are covered under the Dispersed Tribal Development Programme (DTDP).

The rate of literacy among the Scheduled Tribes is 52.24% against the overall literacy rate of 72.87% of the State as per 2011 census. The tribal male and female literacy rates are 63.70% and 41.20% respectively. Over the last decade, there has been a significant improvement in literacy level among the STs in the State, which recorded an increase from 37.37% in 2001 to 52.24% in 2011.

The major educational initiatives of the state Government are:

- Teaching in 10 tribal languages in Primary Schools.

- Pre-Matric scholarship for students staying in the Hostel
- Distribution of free bicycle to SC/ST students (for class-X)
- Free uniform to all.
- Facilitate education for ST students in English Medium schools
- Stipends and scholarships are awarded to tribal children of general schools, colleges and also in the tribal schools run by government.
- Separate hostels, Free and compulsory education with Mid-Day Meal provision
- They are also given training in vocational courses.
- Pre-examination training to prepare students for different administrative examination.
- District wise prizes for the first three tribal students
- Provision of laptops, bicycles, post-matric scholarship to students pursuing higher education.
- Coaching for entrance examination to Engineering and Medical colleges, Civil Services Examination, Banking, Railways etc.

The Constitution of India incorporate several special provisions for the promotion of educational and economic interest of STs. Most of the criticisms of the activities of the Central Government also hold good in the context of Orissa. Besides, the following points of criticism need mention. Little progress seems to have been made in the education of tribals, despite efforts by the Government, such as the establishment of many separate schools for tribal pupils. As is seen from the Table 2.1 the growth of literacy among tribals is very marginal, and in some tribes the literacy rate has actually decreased (e.g. the Parajas). While devising remedies for this problem, the real issues are not touched upon, rather the complex problems are over simplified and solutions offered which are only palliatives and do not deal with underlying causes. The attempt to solve the problem of extensive dropouts among tribal students by extending their stipends for another year in case of failure will not be effective until the deeper causes are identified. Tribal schools, to which the tribal population has undoubtedly responded well, are based on wrong principle of 'separate but equal'.

The STs & SCs Development, Minorities & Backward Classes Welfare Department imparts training to matriculate and Intermediate teachers for tribal schools. But the courses of study are in no way different from the courses of other general training schools. The curriculum does not include the study of tribal culture, customs or languages, which can be of great use to the teachers who teach tribal students. Moreover, holistic approach have not yet been taken or formulated to address the real issues of tribal apathy to education, more importantly to the medium of instruction which is alien and unrelated to their tribal language. Nothing or very little has been done to formulate adaptable language teaching method for shy-out learners. Besides, adequate measures have not yet been taken for their motivation to realize importance or prospects of English language.

Most of the government activities are confined to socio-economic aspects of tribal life and little has been done for the development of their language and culture. There has been little attempt to adapt the schools to the needs of tribals. The design of the buildings, the dress of the teachers, the charts and pictures on the walls, the medium of instruction, the games are all alien to the tribal learner. Instead of becoming an extension of the tribal home and environment, the school is often hostile to tribal traditions. The Government of Odisha has recently started to impart education in one tribal language. The existing text books also create cultural problems for tribal students which will be discussed in the subsequent chapters. No one seems to consider whether the education imparted today is instrumental in destroying the social fabric of the tribals. All these ethnocentric approaches to their education seem to be hastening the process of "detribalization

India, with its innumerable language families, ethnic groups and cultural patterns, presents a unique case of cultural pluralism. The existence of the caste system, which is again unique to India, poses special problems in the education of its disadvantaged" and ethnic groups of learners. *Caste,* observes Lawton, *is the most rigid form of stratification, i.e. mobility from one level in society to another is extremely difficult, if not theoretically impossible: individuals are born into a position in the hierarchy, roles are ascribed rather than achieved; and caste is frequently justified on religious beliefs.* In India, the caste system is justified on religious grounds and caste system, not class system, is the basic principle of social structure.

As suggested by Lewis and Massed, English can be studied on any one of three socio-historical levels. First, it is the traditional language of countries like England, U.S.A. and Australia as well as parts of Canada. Second, it is an ex-colonial language in countries like India and some African nations where the indigenous languages have remained strong. Here it continues to be used but in partnership with the indigenous languages and plays an important part in fundamental education. Third, it is one of the major "languages of wider communication" and thus plays an important role in higher education, particularly, in science and technology. Due to the long colonial rule, the English language is in a 'may-not-be-native-and-yet-may-not-be-foreign-either', relationship to India. It has become the language of the elite. Reacting to the suggestion of introducing other foreign languages in place of English, Dr.Suniti Kumar Chatterjee states: *English is now the most important European language, or world language for the matter of that, and fortunately, as there is in India more than a century old tradition of English Studies and there is the atmosphere of English, it is comparatively easier for us to learn it than any other foreign language. That being so, I would suggest that in our education there must be a place for English.*

The existence of Indo-Anglican literature and its appreciable growth proves that English has become a part of the Indian ethos. Realizing its practical value in the Indian context, almost all the Education Commissions stress its importance for Indian education. In higher education in India, particularly, in science and technology,

English is the medium of instruction and it forms a major subject in selection tests for any Class I or II positions in the Central Government.

Interviews and viva voce tests are also conducted in English and for tribal candidates this will be the case for a long time to come. In this context, the tribals' need for English is greater. The students of post-graduate level were interviewed with three questions regarding their aim/ambition in life, the opportunities available and the major obstacle in their career goal. It was observed that the aim of the students vary in accordance to their ambition, background and upbringing. However, they all dream of a life of comfort for themselves and their family. They are aware that plenty of opportunities are available to them both in Government and non-Government sectors. The major obstacle that they face in achieving their career goal is their lack of communication in English. They also are aware that the students who get selected in interviews are better to them only in communicating the ideas properly to the interviewers.

The answers and opinion of two students are referred below.

No1. My aim in life that I want to become a English Lectuare.

No2 I have got an opportunity for higher study in KISS institute, BBSK.

No3 The major obstacles in acheving my goal in life are the following

- Lack of English Knowledge. Due to lack of English Knowledge I can't appeared in interview because every interview are conducted in English.

- Lack of english in my life, mainly I have not aware about in the English language from Initial point. So I have not good in english language. So I face many problems in English.

1) To Becarne an English Professor. This is my aim in my life.

2) I have got an Great oppertunity For higher education in this institution.

3). The major obstractes in achieving in my life These are follow :-

- Lack of English knowledge due to Not Interested in english Language
- I can't appread an Interview because every interviewer ask in English.
- Lack of Intension in English Language
- I Live in poor village, there fore no facility about English coaching.
- dueto Lack of money not going to English Coaching.

Further, as reported by the *Harijan* and *Adibasi* Commission 1978-79, higher education among tribals and their representation in the Class I Central Government Services, which require such higher education, are far from satisfactory. The problems they face in learning English may be one of the causes for their lagging behind. Learning English aids the tribal children in furthering their studies and enhancing their employability. The fear of learning English – a foreign language, is one of the factors attributed to their backwardness in education, because English language is a criterion rather than an option in higher education.

Odisha State occupies a distinct place in our country as it represents a unique blend of unity amidst diversity. There are 62 Scheduled Tribe communities, each one different from the other. The State has the privilege of having highest number (13) of

Particularly Vulnerable Tribal Groups (PVTGs). The ST population constitutes 22.85% of the total population of the State (as per 2011 census).

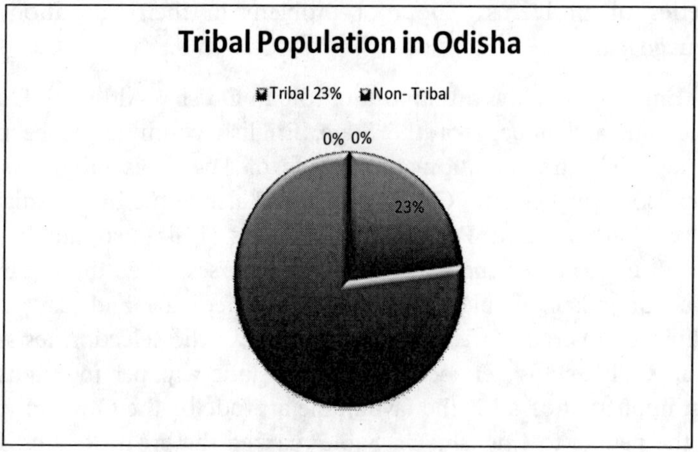

Figure No. 2.2: Tribal Population in Odisha

The State of Odisha has secured important place in the country having a high concentration of Scheduled Tribe and Scheduled Caste population. As per the latest 2011 census, it is ranked third (numerically) in terms of ST population whereas its position is eleventh (numerically) in terms of SC population in the country. Scheduled Tribes and Scheduled Castes together constitute nearly 40% of the State's Total Population (S.Ts 22.85% and S.Cs 17.13%). The population of Scheduled Tribes and Scheduled Castes is as follows:

Table No: 2.1 Scheduled Tribe Population in Odisha

Total Population of Odisha	4,19,74,218
Scheduled Tribes (S.T.) Population	95,90,756
Percentage Of S.T. Population	22.85
S.T. Communities	17.13

The STs are inhabited mostly in the remote parts of the state where there is a lack of all basic amenities which are easily available to the general people. When it comes to education, they have to face varieties of problems. The root problem in their education is language learning.

English still plays an important role in Odisha. Although Odia is the official language of the State, English continues to be the language of administration and courts of law. It is taught as a compulsory subject from Class IV to X and also at the Intermediate, Under Graduate and Post Graduate levels. It is also taught in Agriculture, Engineering and Pharmacy Courses. Even though it is not a compulsory subject in colleges of Medicine and Law, the medium of instruction is English. Besides, all the selection tests in Group C, B and A services generally include a paper in English. Most important of all is the favourable attitude of the Government and the people to English. Dr. Sable marked the great demand for English education in Odisha and was surprised to find the Government subsidizing generously to the Society of the Sisters of Saint Joseph for establishing a Convent School at Bhubaneswar, at a time when Government schools in Bhubaneswar and Odisha lacked adequate financial support. What he speaks of the need for English in Bhubaneswar is also true for the whole of Orissa. To quote him:

> To be excluded from English medium education is not only to be excluded from the most academically sound schooling in Bhubaneswar and from development of fluency in Written and Spoken English, both of which can have enormous effects on chances for future higher and professional education. It is also to be excluded from early acquisition of the language, manners and psychological identity of India's English speaking national elite. (p.73)

Since English plays so important a role in Odisha, proficiency in English is a must for the tribals, particularly for technical studies and for higher jobs where the tribals have a very poor representation.

3

Language through Literature

This chapter is devoted to survey. It has two major sub-section, the first section is devoted to survey of literature in teaching of English with special reference to teaching poetry. Most of the world's literatures had their origins in poems. Poems are, therefore, the first forms of literature to come into being. And teaching of language started with teaching of original pieces of literature, a major part of which constituted poems. To start with, the young learners had problem in comprehending long and difficult original pieces of writings of great writers. The result was memorization. And memorization was considered the most important method of learning. Those who could memorize were considered good learners. Poetry, because of its rhyme and mnemonic value, was considered to be the best, from the point of view of both the teachers and the learners. As often texts were not available, to begin with, the teacher could teach from his/her memory and the learners could commit them to memory. Thus poetry was the best bait for teaching. With the colonization of most of the countries by the English and the settlement of English people in countries like America, Australia and New Zealand, teaching of English became a part and parcel of education of many counties of the world. And, to begin with, the teaching of English in those Countries began with teaching of English Literature. And learning English culture and English social and literature history were considered inseparable part of studying English. However, planting of English in different parts of the world slowly resulted in different varieties of English which, in turn, resulted in varieties of English literatures such as

American literature, Common Wealth literature, Indian English literature, etc. Teaching of English literature, with initial hiccups, embraced with some degree of reluctance, the teaching of these varieties, English literature and the varieties of English.

With the increase of science and technology, trade and commerce, international transport and communication, the world has become a global village and English its language. With this changed scenario, the needs and the purposes of learning English and studying only English literature does not serve these purposes. Hence the focus in teaching English has shifted from teaching English literature to teaching English language resulting in the emergence of ELT. During the last 3-4 decades ESP (English for Specific Purposes)is in the process of taking over ELT and has pushed teaching of English literature to a very restricted place-a branch of ESP i.e. ELP (English for Literary Purposes). Thus, currently a very insignificant number of learners of the world learn English for developing literary skills but most of them learn English for developing English language skills often related to their on-job requirements.

Because of socio-economic and cultural differences, education in Western developed countries is, in many ways, different from education in Third World countries. The large classes, poor infrastructure, problem of over-population make India's education very different from Western Countries where English is mainly taught as mother tongue and in very comfortable circumstances. Besides, we mostly use old traditional methods and approaches in teaching/learning of English. If it is language based, then our approach is still grammar and structure-based. If literature-based, we mainly teach literature of English in very traditional ways. Third World countries, particularly, countries which were under long British rule, have a very strong tradition of teaching English literature. Teaching literature needs a base of general English skill, and most of these Third World countries switched over to mother tongue as their medium of instruction. The English standard of students, after this transition, deteriorated very basic skills of English. Thus teaching of Shakespeare or Wordsworth was questioned because most of the students fail to agree their verbs with the nouns. As a result, the movement of 'language through literature' gained ground. The English courses became more language-oriented.

Thus, in Third World countries, like India two approaches prevail-such as literature for literature and language through literature. In lower classes of English, particularly at the school and tertiary level, the approach is mainly teaching English language through literature and at the higher classes, at the degree college and post-graduate level, the approach is dominated by teaching English literature. Rightly understood, literature and language are two parts of the same coin and adopting an approach of golden mean both literary and language skill can be developed in the learners through teaching of literature. Carter insists that a natural resolution would be to take an approach in which language and literature teaching are more closely integrated and harmonized than is commonly, the case at the present time so that literature would not be isolated, possibly rejected, on account of the "literariness" of its language. It is worth quoting his words here:

> It is my contention that some of the language activities and work with models on the literariness of text can aid such development, and that response to and confidence in working with a language using a variety of integrated activities, with language based hypotheses and in classes where investigative, student-centred learning is the norm.

But unfortunately, in India, these two approaches are viewed as two mutually opposed approaches often dividing the supporters and practitioners of these two group into two combating camps. Fortunately, in Western countries like America, England and European countries, the dominate, or even the only mode, is teaching language. Teaching English literature is confined to only some departments of English of some Universities, where the students specialize in studying literature as a subject of higher research or study courses like creative writing to take up writing in English as a profession.

In Odisha, English is taught as a foreign language and the teaching starts from the primary level (Class III). The current English textbooks in school mainly focus on language teaching-not language through literature for which anthologies are more in use than course books as textbooks of English. English teaching in Odisha is beset with a multiplicity of problems such as lack of adequate number of qualified teachers, non-availability of textbooks and in-service training in ELT, unsuitable pre-service training, a highly expensive and ambitious set of culturally-alien textbooks and utter lack of work culture or professionalism on the part of teachers of English. Students, thus, come to college (about 90% of them) without achieving the English language skills of the first year of learning English.

The existing English text books in Odisha reflect middle or upper middle class culture and values and serve primarily to prepare middle or upper class children to participate in their own cultural ethos. The 'text book families', with their customs and traditions and the pictorial illustrations and concepts used in the text lessons are alien to tribal pupils. Students belonging to middle and higher classes, already trained at home in this culture, find no difficulty in following these books and the school becomes a constitution of the home for them.

But for tribal pupils who are already at a disadvantage with regard to language education and are struggling to acquire basic competence in even the regional language, the English textbook and the class appear quite alien and complex. What the pupils have learned at home is of little use to them and they have to learn everything anew. Tribal children do not grow up in families and settings such as those described in these textbooks. Their home is often overcrowded, without the basic amenities of life. I do not mean that English textbooks should depict only tribal families and reflect tribal culture. What I mean is that the culture gap should be less and attempts should be made to make the contexts appear less foreign to tribal pupils. This could have been done easily for states with considerable tribal populations when they adapted these books for their schools. But little has been done to reduce the cultural gap.

The Board of Writers and Editors appointed by the Government of Odisha, for instance, where tribals and Scheduled Castes constitute forty percent of the population, has done nothing.

The tribals who live in different cultural settings have more difficulties in learning a foreign language. Their mother tongue is referred to as *Adivasi Bhasa*. This wide gap between the culture reflected in the English textbooks and the culture of the tribal pupils develops a negative self-image and the sense of inferiority among them. The existing English textbooks, in other words, contribute to "detribalization". To check this tendency, the materials used should avoid situations which make tribal pupils feel uneasy and ashamed of their own background. When these cultural differences are negligible, the teacher's explanations can help tribal pupils in understanding the context. But when the difference is high, the teacher's explanation is not very useful or effective. If attempts are not made to suit the English texts to the tribal pupil, the English class might trigger dropouts among them (which is already the case) and kill the tribal pupil's pleasure in learning English. Unless this cultural impasse is first resolved and removed, any attempt to teach them English will be of little value.

Poetry or songs are the first form of literature that a child gets acquainted with, when after birth the mother lulls the baby with a lullaby. Even before a child learns the alphabets, he/she gets acquainted with songs and more often than not it gets committed to his/her memory, unaware.

For the tribal learners in specific, they are more acquainted with songs than the general learners. Songs are an important part of their day-to-day communication and celebration, even though, many of them are illiterate and have no scripts of their own.

Short stories and plays with themes familiar to their culture can definitely help in improving their learning but, poetry has an advantage over them for its short length, simple themes, rhythm and capacity for quick memorization.

Literature, as stated before, started with poetry and teaching of literature started with teaching of poetry. Both the approaches-such as teaching literature and teaching Language (or Language through literature) – by and large depend on poems as teaching materials for the following reasons:

1. It helps student understand and appreciate cultures and beliefs different from their own. By constructing with the literary text a reality different from that of tests of information, students are given access to a world of attitudes, and values, collective imaginings and historical frames of reference that constitute the memory of people or speech community. Thus literature and culture are inseparable. (Kramsch: 1992, p.175)
2. Poetry can serve as an example of certain types of language patterns and structures (Like vocabulary usage and syntax). Literature also provides a rich context in which individual lexical or syntactical items are made more memorable. Reading a substantial and contextual body of text, students gain familiarity with many features of the written language-like the formation and function of sentences, the varieties of possible structures, the different ways of connecting ideas. Poems can serve as an excellent prompt for oral work(Collie & Salter, 1987; Mackay, 1986)
3. Poetry deals with universal themes that are familiar to all cultures such as love, nature, children, animals, sea, friendship, society, wars, etc. (Maley & Duff, 1989)
4. Literature, more particularly poetry, is language in context. They are authentic materials and so the use of poetry brings in context to the classroom. (Sharma, 2006).
5. Poems offer a rich and, varied repertoire and are a source of much enjoyment for teacher and learner alike. They often explore them of universal concern and embody life experiences, observations and the feelings evoked by them. Reading poetry enables the learner to experience the power

of language outside the strait-jacket of more standard written sentence structure and lexis. In the classroom, using poetry can lead naturally on to freer, creative written expression. Indeed, poems are capable of producing strong response from the reader, and this memorable intensity motivates further reading of poetry in the foreign language. (Collie &Salter: 226)

6. Spiro (2004) holds that the typical features of poetry make it very suitable for language teaching. She points out that controlled language practice shares certain features with poetry. There is repetition and pattern (for example, in oral and written drills of grammar structures and in gap filling) or substitution exercises in which learners use given patterns as models for other sentences. Also, the length of text in a poem is usually short, as is text we use for controlled language practice, the learner is encouraged 'to be creative and to use strategies for applying the familiar to the unfamiliar – just as poets do. (Spiro:7)

But there seem to have big differences between literature and language through literature approaches of teaching poems with regard to definition of poems, the purposes of teaching poems, the methods of teaching poems, etc. The table below provides some of these points of differences:

Table No. 3.1 Comparison of the Literature Approach & Language Approach

Literature Approach	Language Approach
Purpose is developing literary skills.	Purpose is developing literary and language skills.
Criteria of selections of Poems are narrow. Often English poems of great Poets of England with great literary value are chosen.	Criteria of selections of Poems are broad. English poems of any country or nationality, not strictly on the basis of literary value.
Poems are often taught in relation to the poet and the age.	Poems are often taught without referring to the poet and the age.
Method used is lecture oriented, teaching through explanation.	Method used is learner centered approach, interactive approach –

	through no or very little explanation.
No language activities	Lots of language activities
Test is mostly through long-type questions and/or annotation of passage.	Test is mostly through language activities, Language-Focus questions; short answer type questions.
Hardly any writing tasks are given; Little or no feedback	Lots of written tasks are given; detail feedback given to help learners learn language.
Do not consider songs / nursery rhymes as poems.	Use a lot of action song/nursery rhymes to teach the beginners.

Kalinga Institute of Social Sciences (KISS), is the largest tribal residential institution in the world. It has been glorifying the capital, the state and the country quite consistently. With an humble beginning at 1993 with only 193 tribal children of primary classes, it has reached to an unbelievable strength of 30,000 children studying from class KG to Post-doctoral level. KISS has been providing facilities like food, cloth, education, stationery, medical facilities etc. all free of cost. The foundation of KISS stands on some definite missions which has made it grow so strong and so high. Some of them include eradication of poverty and empowerment through education, transformation of 'liability' to 'asset', mainstreaming the tribal population, to provide them a better life and to use them as 'change agents' and uplift their status in the society. Not only this, KISS has been providing 'earning while learning' facility to every students through compulsory vocational education so that they will be self-dependent in the society. Every year the meritorious students of KISS get an opportunity to pursue higher professional education at different institutions of KIIT. This will also contribute to the lessening of anti-social activities. Apart from that, they are also benefitted by the facilities provided by the government.

The unique feature of KISS is that while it has been successfully mainstreaming the tribal students, it has taken all care to retain their own unique culture. They are given every opportunity to observe all of their festivals with all customary inside the campus, they dance and sing to the tune of their own beautiful songs and at the same time they have glorified Institution's fame by securing seats at institutes of international repute like IIT, NIT, IIM; grabbing jobs at TCS, WIPRO, Cognizant and so many MNCs and PSUs.

The two years' Higher Secondary course at KISS is registered under the Department of School and Mass Education, Government of Odisha. The books prescribed by the Government are taught in KISS. There are four books in English, Invitation to English 1, 2, 3, 4. The first book contains prose and poetry, the second book contains non-detailed stories, third book deals with writing skills and the last with grammar. So far the proficiency of the students in English language is concerned, they are found to be very poor. Surprisingly, they are average and better in other subjects but have a special alienation and phobia towards English. They try to acquire just pass marks and never aspire for more. On survey, it was revealed that the time they enter into the first year of college, they have not acquired adequate knowledge they should have by that time. The main reason behind a low level of proficiency in English, as stated by them, being that English being fourth language for many of them, it has become an extra burden and they only aim to get a pass percentage in it. Though many of them aim to pursue higher education, preferably technical, they could now realize that knowledge in English will be a great help to achieve their goals. Learning English will definitely help them in furthering their studies and enhancing their employment opportunity.

4

Evaluation

The field survey has two components – Evaluation of the poetry course and the evaluation of the teaching of Poetry through administration of questionnaires to both the teachers and student.

The two years Intermediate (or Higher Secondary class) has English as a compulsory subject. It aims at improving their basic English language learning through the four skills of listening, speaking, reading, and writing. A close examination at the first year of the 2 years' syllabus shows that it has poems ranging from American poet like Robert Frost's *Stopping By Woods on a Snowy Evening* to Irish poet Thomas Moore's *Oft in the Stilly Nights*; English poet Robert Southey's *The Inchcape Rock* to Indian poet Gopa Ranjan Mishra's *Fishing* and Elizabeth Pinrad's *To My True Friend.* The themes range from romantic poem depicting natural beauty to description on true friendship; about the agony of old age to a story about a sea pirate; and the merciful act involved in fishing. Each poem is divided into sections like 'Introducing the Poet' in some poems where a brief background of the poet is given. 'Warm Up' section gives an introduction on the poem; then comes the 'Text' which is followed by 'Glossary' where the meanings of difficult words are given. Finally the 'Think it Out' section asks questions on the poem.

So as to analyze the relevance of the present prescribed materials in poetry for tribal learners, the researcher has tried to evaluate the five poems as discussed below:

Name of the Poem: Fishing
Poet: Gopa Ranjan Mishra

The selection of the poem "Fishing" for class XI is good as it suits to the level of the learners, particularly tribal learners. The language is simple except for some words. The theme is also appropriate for tribal learners. But, it seems that the editors have failed to visualize how the teacher is going to use the poem in the classroom to help the tribal learners understand and enjoy the poem and at the same time-learn English.

The lesson is not clearly divided into three sections – pre-reading, while-reading and post-reading. The "Warm up" serves as a pre-reading activity. But there is not any activity rather the central theme of the poem is mentioned in two lines. The act through which the objective is achieved has not been discussed. Moreover, a brief introduction of the poet should have been there.

Notes and Glossary

This section is inadequate. Meaning of 'feat', 'fervent'. 'lo', 'popped', 'wriggled', 'gasping', 'wistful', 'den', 'mocking', 'crimson' are not mentioned. Moreover the different usages (like verb, noun) should be mentioned.

Think it out

Question 1 (What idea of the speaker's age do you find in the first line?) seems irrelevant and should be removed as it has nothing to do with the ultimate objective of the poem. Question 4 (Describe his initial experience-lns.9-12) is confusing and tribal learning learners may find it difficult to express. Question 8 (Describe the catch) may appear difficult to the learners due to the use of the word 'catch'. Similarly question 10 (What did he think the fish was pleading for?) may be difficult for the presence of the word 'pleading'. Question 12 (Discuss the significance of: "For nothing, however, I did care"), question 13 (What was the strange feeling that the speaker felt? Can you relate the feeling to the "crimson glow" and "greater joy"?-lns. 36-38) and question 14 (Which action brought about a greater joy in the heart of the speaker? In comparison to the ultimate greater joy, what do you think would have been a lesser happiness?) are difficult for the students to analyse and answer. Question 13 (What was the strange feeling that the speaker felt? Can you relate the feeling to the "crimson glow" and "greater joy"? – lns. 36-38) and 15 (Why does he find this feeling strange?) will have almost the same answer. In question 16 (Do you think the speaker was sensitive? Why do you think so? Clue: atleast two reason) the use of the word 'sensitive' is difficult for the learners as they don't know the meaning of the word and its usages. Moreover there is no clue given.

Poem-Oft, In The Stilly Night
Poet-Thomas Moore

The selection of the poem for students of class XI is good and a nostalgic one for the learners. The language is not that difficult. The theme is appropriate for students, particularly for those who are staying away from their native place. But the way it has been presented in the book, the activities and the question doesn't seem engrossing for all the learners. It lacks in activities and descriptions to create interest among the students so as to make effective learning.

Introduction of the Poet

In introducing the poet, it is written that he is an Irish poet, satirist, composer and political propagander. The adjectives used in describing the poet is quite difficult for many non-tribal students, leave alone tribals. So a slightly easier adjectives could have been used for the purpose else it rests on the teachers will to explain them or leave them.

Warm Up

Summaries the poem in one line. It gives a good description in the shortest possible way. But here many questions can be asked to the students regarding their own experience of their childhood memories and friends; they can be asked to narrate the nostalgic moments which they have witnessed, of their grandparents or other elderly people around them. This could have helped the learners to relate to the emotions felt by the poet in the poem.

Glossary

Glossary describes the meaning of only six words whereas for tribal students many difficult words are there such as 'fond', 'dimm'd', 'ere', 'deserted', 'garlands' etc. the use of words like 'deserted' should have been followed by its use both as noun and verb with some more examples like that.

Think It Out

There are seven questions in the 'think it out' section. The first question is quite confusing as the answers may vary from 'old age' to 'night'. In question no 6 and 7, there are questions on 'figures of speech' like 'similies' and 'personification'. The teacher needs to explain to the students details on them and should help identify them in the poem while teaching. Otherwise it would be quite difficult to answer those questions.

Poem-Stopping By Woods on a Snowy Evening
Poet-Robert Frost

The selection of the poem for class XI is good and it is an inspiring poem for the learners. The language is quite simple except for some archaic. The theme is also appropriate for young learners. But the way it needs to be presented in the class (as described in the text book) does not seem appropriate so as to cater to the understanding of tribal learners. It also has no descriptions in order to answer the readers and learn language through it.

The lesson is not clearly divided into three sections, i.e. pre-reading, while-reading and post-read ingactivities. There is an introduction to the author and 'warm up' section which serves as pre-reading activities. But there is no activity or introductory questions in it except the theme which has been introduced in two sentences.

Notes and Glossary

This section appears sufficient for a small poem. Different usages of the words like noun, verb should have been there.

Think it Out

Question no. 1 (How is 'woods' different from 'forest' appears confusing as they have lived mostly in the dense forest areas and finds it difficult to distinguish between the two. Question no. 4 ('He will not see me stopping here' – what does this expression mean?) is also absurd to ask to tribal learners because for the tribal people, woods/ forests belong to the almighty and no one in particular has its ownership. Same can be stated for question no 8 where the reaction of the owner of the woods and the horse towards the natural beauty of the woods is questioned. Even the expression "the darkest evening of the year" in question no 10 is also confusing as the areas where the tribal live is dark in the evening throughout the year due to lack of electricity.

Post-reading Activities: The first question of this activity has given jumbled up sentences to describe the theme of the poem and the learners will arrange them in the correct sequence. This activity is quite alright but among those six sentences, nowhere the owner of the woods is hinted at. So the learner may get confused at the importance given to the owner in the very beginning of the poem. The second question asking the rhyme scheme is irrelevant for the tribal learners as they have no theoretical knowledge of the rhyme scheme beforehand.

Poem-The Inchcape Rock
Poet-Robert Southey

This is a very long poem with sixteen stanzas. Though it is quite interesting with a great moral, the tribal students found it difficult to understand. This poem describes the mis-adventorous life of Sir Ralph, the Rover who is punished at the end by the supreme power for his evil deeds. But the poetic description of the natural scenic background is beyond the understanding of tribals of Odisha. It is mainly because they mostly inhabit the hills and forests which are far away from the sea coast. Besides such ship pirates are hardly seen in the state coasts. So they find it difficult to relate quickly to the theme. Moreover the poem is too long and divided into three units which makes it boring at times.

Unit-I

Glossary contains only four words where as there are many other words which are beyond the tribal students' understanding. Words like stir and perilous are not described which should have been given. The questions in the Think It Out section are alright but appears difficult for the understanding of the tribals.

Unit-II

The Warm Up in Unit-II contains some words and descriptions which needs further explanation (mischief, malice). In the second Unit, glossary is missing with words like screamed, joyance, deck, wickedness, Quoth, gurgling etc. Again the questions here are beyond the level of understanding of the tribal students.

Unit-III

The Warm Up in Unit III has words like recoils, sinner which need clarification. The glossary doesn't consist of words like scoured, plundered, hath, dawn, roar, methinks, shone, drift, vessel, strikes, shivering, despair, sinking, beneth, dreadful and knell. Similarly the questions too need further clarification to enable the tribal students to answer them.

Poem-To My True Friend
Poet-Elizabeth Pinard

'To My True Friend' is a long poem of eleven stanzas written by Elizabeth Pinrad. The theme of the poem is based on the true friendship of poet and her friend. It is quite appropriate for the students of class XI and they can easily relate to the descriptions given in the poem. But there is no activities given in the text books which will help the teacher in giving an idea of the theme as pre-reading. It is quite inappropriate to directly jump to the poem and start teaching even a simple theme like this. The words in the poem are simple except a few.

Warm-Up

There is no introduction of the poet and the editors felt to do away with it. Only there is some description on friendship and its place in one's life.

Glossary

The glossary is too short with only three phrases described in it. The tribal students found it difficult to understand the words like 'sorrow', 'circumstances', 'treasured',; precious', 'flourishes', 'infinity', 'bliss' etc. uses like 'as....as (as dark as night..)' can also be elaborated in the glossary.

Think it Out

There are ten questions in total. They all seem alright for students except question no 3,4 and 5. The tribal students found it difficult and confusing to answer these questions as they appear almost the same.

The researcher has observed six classes of English poetry at KISS. The method is lecture-oriented. Almost all the teachers are found to start with a brief introduction to the poet and his/her age and then proceed to explaining the poem and analyzing it. Some started introducing the poem in an interesting way such as writing few lines and asking students to guess what is the poem about. Some others ask questions about the poem before explaining it, but finally they explain the poem and students passively listen.

The most important task of the teachers seemed to be explaining the meanings of difficult words as every alternative word seems to be difficult for the students. Most of the learners' time and energy, therefore, is spent in writing the meanings of these words in Odia.

The questions in any poetry test of any poem has three forms: explanation of extracts from poems already taught to the students. Most of the questions have 3-4 sentences answers. Many of the teachers did not have time to discuss questions in one period of 1 hour duration. Majority of the time was devoted in explaining the poem. The students could not answer the questions in full sentences as it required them to frame long sentences. However, some of them could answer Yes/No type questions. Moreover, when they were asked to write the answers, their writing was much below satisfaction. Though they seemed to have understood the poem, they fail to answer the questions either orally or in writing. Here is a scanned copy of an answer sheet of a student.

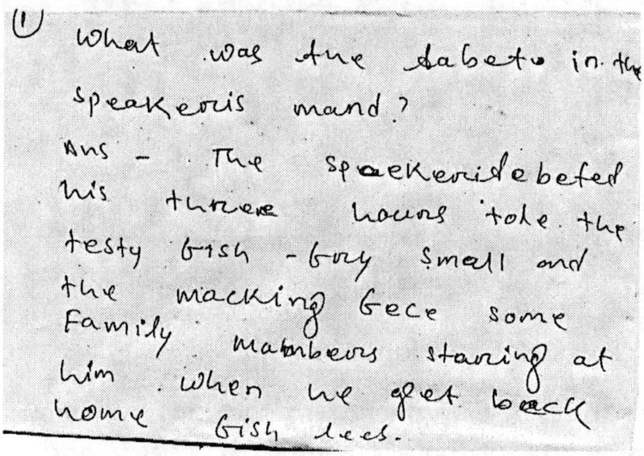

(1) What was the dabeto in the speakeris mand?

Ans – The speakeridebefed his threre hours tole the testy bish – bry small and the macking bece some family mabnbeors staring at him when he get back home bish lees.

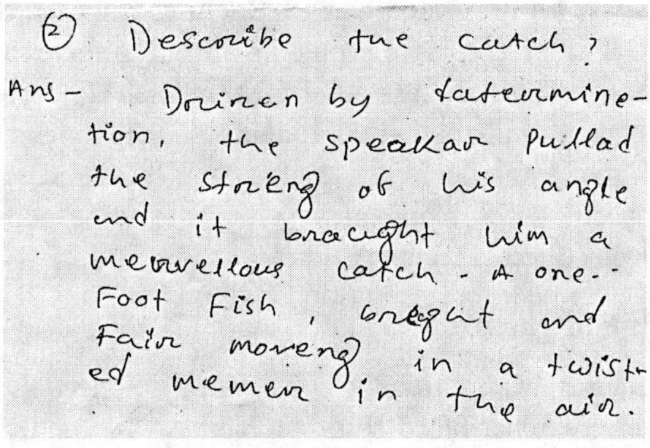

(2) Describe the catch?

Ans – Driven by dateormine-tion, the speakar pullad the stroeng of his angle end it braught him a merrvellous catch – A one-foot fish, bregut and fair moveng in a twist-ed memer in the air.

The scripts are also evaluated mechanically. Student's errors were not underlined and no feedback given. Stated below a part of an examined script from a mid-term test in which the examiner is expected to point out the errors and provide feedback to the learners to help his/her English improve. The script will also throw light on the average learner's level of English and how they mug up answers for exam.

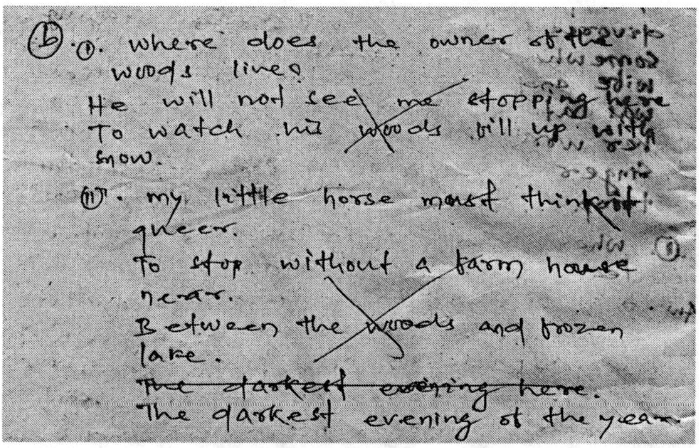

(b) (i). where does the owner of the woods lives.
He will not see me stopping here
To watch his woods fill up with snow.
(ii). my little horse must think queer.
To stop without a farm house near.
Between the woods and frozen lake.
~~The darkest evening here.~~
The darkest evening of the year.

Field Survey Through Questionnaire

Preparing an anthology of poems for the low-proficient students implies investigation of both teaching of poetry and language teaching to devise an integrated way of teaching language through poems. Two questionnaires have been constructed to serve the study purpose-one for students and the other for teachers. 120 copies have been distributed among first year students of Higher Secondary class of KISS, and another seven to the faculty members at the Dept. Of English, KISS. Bhubaneswar and the same number of copies have been collected back.

The Student's Questionnaire

The questionnaires were carefully constructed to meet the study purposes. The researcher faced some problems while putting forth the project. Some of the students were careless in their responses to the questionnaire. The questionnaire included questions and sub-questions.

Description of the Questionnaire

The questionnaire has three sections

Section I is devoted to personal information about the students. Section II gives an idea on general information on poetry that are taught to the students, the student's opinions about poems that are prescribed, and the percentage of how much they can understand poems without the help of their teachers. Section III aims at giving an insight-through the students-about the method the teacher employ while teaching a poem. The questionnaire is available in Appendix A.

The students' questionnaire, as stated above, covers three sections: section I gives information about the student. They had freedom to answer the questions as per their personal opinion. Some of the questions of section I are about the tribal's association with poetry in their day-to-day life. The questions in Section I are as follows:

Question no 1 to 5 was all about their personal information like Name, Class/stream, Section, Tribe and District. In the subsequent questions about their tribal language as mother tongue, 104 out of 120 students (approximately 86%) said that they have their indigenous tribal language as mother tongue but their language has no script of it's own. 60% of the students said that they communicate both in their own language and Odia language and 40% communicate in their tribal language only. When asked the age in which they started to learn their tribal language, all of them answered that they started to learn it at the first year of their life where as they learnt Odia at the age of 3 and English at 10 or 11. They were asked about their likeness towards music and songs. All of them answered in affirmative and 80% of them can sing songs in their own tribal language. They also said that they have different songs specified for different occasions and they like singing in day-to-day life. They use riddles in their daily conversation.

Some questions of section II are as follows:

Q1. What subjects do you study?

The options provided are:

a) Prose

b) Poetry

c) Non-detail

d) Writing and Grammar

e) All of the above

All of them answered the last option i.e. all the given subjects.

Q2. Which of them do you think easy and interesting for you?

a) Prose

b) Poetry

c) Non-detail

d) Writing and Grammar

e) All of the above

Only seventeen students among 120 have found Grammar easy and interesting, While most of them have found non-detail and poetry to be an easy and interesting subject.

Q3. Which is difficult and uninteresting?

Most of the students have found writing skills to be difficult and uninteresting. However, the second rank is received by both poetry and grammar alike, the two subjects that are most disliked by the students.

Q4. Which subject do you prefer?

Prose Or Poetry

Around 85% opined that they personally prefer Prose.

Q5. Do you remember any poem that you were taught in high school?

a) Yes (90%) (b) No (10%)

Q6. Do you remember it's name? (a) Yes (b) No

Name of the poem

All of them were able to write one name.

Q7. Rate the poems you are taught

a) Stopping by Woods on a Snowy Evening
   1. Difficult 2.Easy 3.Old 4.Boring 5.Interesting
b) Oft, In the Stilly Night
   1. Difficult 2.Easy 3.Old 4.Boring 5.Interesting
c) The Inchcape Rock
   1. Difficult 2.Easy 3.Old 4.Boring 5.Interesting
d) To My True Friend
   1. Difficult 2.Easy 3.Old 4.Boring 5.Interesting
e) Fishing
   1. Difficult 2.Easy 3.Old 4.Boring 5.Interesting

Opinions	Number of students	Percentage
Difficult	58	48.33%
Easy	9	7.55%
Old/Archaic	22	18.33%
Interesting	14	11.66%
Boring	17	14.16%

Approximately 50% of the students find poetry difficult. Just a few students find poetry easy and interesting.

Q8. If difficult, why do you think difficult?

a) Words difficult b) Theme is difficult c) Very long

90% of the students opined that the poems appear difficult because of the difficult words and theme used in it.

Q9. If easy, why do you think easy?

a) Simple language b) Interesting theme c) Short poem

The poems which were easy were actually so because of the easy and simple language used in it, as stated by the students.

Q10. From the poems prescribed for you, how much can you understand on your own without the teachers' help?

a) Only 5% b) 10% to 20% c) 30% to 40% d) 50% to 70%

The students said that they can understand only 5% to 20 % without the help of the teachers.

Teaching Poetry

Q1. What steps does your teacher take to teach you a poem?

a) Does s/he introduce the poem in an interesting way?

b) Does s/he read aloud the poem?

c) Does s/he ask you to read the poem silently for some time?

d) Does s/he ask you questions from the poem?

e) Does s/he give you interesting task/ activities from the poem?

f) Does s/he ask you to do these activities in pair/ group?

It was found that most of the teachers introduce the poem in an interesting way, read the poem aloud, ask the students to read the poem silently and ask questions. But they don't get sufficient time for activities either individually or in group.

Q2. Does s/he explain to you through giving a lecture on the poem and explaining the meaning of the difficult words? (Yes/No)

All the responses were in affirmative.

Q3. While teaching, does s/he move around the class or just stays near the board and explain/ lecture? (Yes/No)

a) Yes-65% (77students) b) No-35% (43 students)

Q4. Does s/he use the blackboard? If yes, to what purpose?

All the teachers use blackboard to explain the meaning of difficult words.

Q5. Who do you consider a good poetry teacher?

a) One who allows you to understand the poem on your own with little help when necessary

Or

b) One who explains the poem through lectures without allowing you to understand on your own.

In students' opinion, the teacher who allows you to understand the poem on your own with little help when necessary is actually a good teacher.

Q6. Does your teacher give you some writing tasks on poems and provide you with feedback? (Yes/No)

a) Yes-33% (40 students) b) No-67% (80 students)

Q7. Does s/he points out your errors and provide you suggestions to improve your English? (Yes/No)

a) Yes-21% (25 students)

b) No-79% (95 students)

Q8. What are the questions on tests should be?

a) Short type b. Long type

All the students opine that the questions should be short type.

Q9. How do you prepare for the exam?

a) Mug up with little understanding

b) Write from memory in your own English

77.5 % (93 students) say that they mug up the answers for examination with little understanding and only 22.5% (27 students) write from their memory.

Q10. Do you feel tensed before examination? (Yes/No)

a) Yes-80% (96 students)

b) No-20% (24 students)

Q11. What would you like? Poetry should be removed from your syllabus?

It should stay but poems which are simple and interesting be included which you can understand on your own with little help from the teacher

All the students want poetry to be a part of their course but it should be selected carefully. They want short, simple and interesting poems in their syllabus.

The Teachers' Questionnaire

Description of the Questionnaire

Seven copies were distributed among seven faculty members and all the copies were collected back. Teacher's questionnaire consists of three sections. Section I is devoted to personal data and their knowledge on tribals, their culture and language. Section II consists of sixteen questions regarding objectives, selection and suggestion for students. Section III also has sixteen questions regarding the method the teacher employs while teaching the poems. The questionnaire is available in Appendix B.

Data Analysis of the Questionnaire

As the respondent's number is only 7, the responses of each of them are provided in detail-serially.

Section I (Personal data)

1. Name:
2. Qualification:

1. M.A
2. M.A, B.Ed, Ph.D (Cont.)
3. M.A, CTE

4. M.A., M.Phil., Ph.D (Cont.).
5. Ph.D.
6. M.A., M.Phil., Ph.D.(Cont.)
7. M.A, B. Ed, Ph.D (Cont.)

All the teachers are well qualified.

Experience of teaching in Higher Secondary level

1. Fifteen years
2. Three years
3. Eighteen years
4. Nine years
5. Fifteen years
6. Five years
7. Eight Years

Their experience range from three to fifteen years.

1. Do you belong to Schedule Tribe?

   None of them belong to Scheduled Tribe community.

2. Are you aware of tribal culture?

   Six teachers said they are aware of tribal culture and only one teacher denied knowing about their culture.

3. Have you got any special training in teaching English? (If yes, mention the kind of training you have got)?

   Except one, all others have been trained in teaching English. Two has got B.Ed and M.Ed degree, One Certificate in Teaching English, two have got training in English Access Micro-Sholarship Programme at KISS under US Embassy, Two are continuing their Post Graduate Diploma in Teaching of English.

4. Have you got any special training in teaching to tribal learners? (If yes, mention the kind of training you have got)?

   None of the teachers have got any special training in teaching to tribal students in specific.

5. Do you know any tribal languages? (if yes, mention the languages)?

   None of them know any tribal language.

6. How is teaching to non-tribal students different from teaching to tribal learners?

   According to them, teaching to tribal students is different from teaching to non-tribal students. They feel that the tribals are slow learners, introvert and never ask questions in class.

7. What according to you is most suitable for teaching to the tribal learners?

   a) Prose b) Poetry c) Non-detail d) Grammar (e) All

   Five out of seven said Non-detail, one said Grammar and One, Poetry.

8. Why do you think so?

   Teaching Non-detail involves story telling which creates interest among them. It has less activities so they fear it the less. It also creates a joyful atmosphere for teaching. Teaching Grammar helps them learn the structure. The teacher who responded with poetry teaching said that it gives the learners scope to think, express and be creative freely.

9. Which form of literature is closely related to tribal life and culture?

   a) Prose b) Poetry c) Non-detail d) Grammar (e) All

Three of the teachers opined for poetry and non-detail, one each for poetry and non-detail alone and two said all the subjects are related to their life.

10. In which language do you communicate with your students in the class?

    (a) English (b) Odia (c) Tribal language (d) specify, if other____________

    Four teachers said that they communicate both in English and Odia, two in English alone and one in Odia alone.

11. In which language do you communicate with your students outside the class?

    (a) English (b) Odia (c) Tribal language (d) specify, if other____________

    Four teachers said that they communicate both in English and Odia, two in English alone and one in Odia alone.

12. Here are some opinions expressed by people about the tribals. How many of them do you consider to be true?

    a) They are ignorant.

    b) Their culture is inferior.

    c) They drink too much.

    d) They are orthodox and superstitious.

    e) They are incapable of mental work.

    f) It is difficult to persuade them.

    g) They are less intelligent.

    h) They are difficult to educate.

    i) They have no idea of cleanliness.

    j) They are lazy and docile.

k) They are quite satisfied with what they have and do not try to improve their lot.

l) They are impulsive, short-tempered and emotional.

m) They are cruel and fond of physical violence.

n) They are cheated easily.

o) They are loose in their moral habits.

p) They lack courtesy.

One faculty member did not attempt this question. The response of others are summarized below.

- Innocence – 5 teachers
- Trust worthy – 4 teachers
- Obedience – 4 teachers
- Orthodox and superstitious – 4 teachers
- Happy-go-lucky attitude – 3 teachers
- Difficult to persuade – 2 teachers
- Less intelligence – 2 teachers
- Quite satisfied – 2 teachers
- Impulsive, short tempered and emotional – 1 teachers
- Cruel, fond of physical violence – 1 teachers
- Easily cheated – 2 teachers
- No trust for non-tribals – 2 teachers

13. What is your opinion in general about the scholastic ability of the tribal students?

a) Most of them do well in their studies as the non-tribal students.

b) They are superior to non-tribal students in studies.

c) They are inferior to the non-tribal students.

Four of them opted for the third option that they are inferior to non-tribal students, two said that they do well in studies than the non-tribal students and one said that they are superior to the non-tribal students.

14. Do you think they have any special educational problems which the non-tribal students don't have?

    Almost all except one said that they have special educational problems.

15. If your answer to the Q No 14 is Yes, what, in your opinion, are the special difficulties that the tribal students have?

    a) Their cultural background comes in the way of their receiving modern education.

    b) The poverty of the tribal students is more acute than that of non-tribal students.

    c) Tribal students don't receive enough encouragement from the society.

    d) Their language problems come in their way of education.

    e) They are inherently lazy and not interested in study.

All the options got equal weightage according to the teachers.

16. Do you feel that your students have special problems in learning English as compared to non-tribal students?

    Yes / No / Not Certain

    All answered in affirmative.

17. If your answer to question No 16 is yes, what are some of the special problems that tribal students have in learning English?

a) The fact that English is third or fourth language for them, where as it is a 2nd or 3rd language for non-tribal students with Odia mother tongue.

b) The fact that most of the tribal students are first generation learners.

c) They have special cultural difficulties.

d) They are poor at learning language in general.

e) They have less motivation in learning English than non-tribals.

f) They have no desire to learn English as they think this will lead to a loss of identity.

g) They have less encouragement from their parents and guardians for learning English than the non-tribal students.

h) They have no idea of the importance of English in the modern world.

According to them, the fact that English is third or fourth language for them, where as it is a 2nd or 3rd language for non-tribal students with Odia mother tongue, most of the tribal students are first generation learners, they get less encouragement from their parents and guardians for learning English than the non-tribal students and have no idea of the importance of English in the modern world, are some of the major problems in their education.

18. Do you think some of the themes and ideas found in the English text books create cultural problems for tribal students?

    Yes / No

    All answered in affirmative.

19. Have you ever felt difficulty in communicating such themes and ideas to them?

Never / Rarely / Often

50% of the teachers said that they often have problems in teaching the tribal students, 30% rarely and 20% never encounter problem while teaching to tribal students.

20. Do you think that knowing their culture and language will be an advantage to you in teaching them English?

Yes / No

All answered in affirmative.

General Poetry

1. What subjects do you teach?

a) Prose

b) Poetry

c) Non-detail

d) Writing and Grammar

e) All of the above

All the teachers teach all the subjects.

2. Which of them do you think easy and interesting for you to teach?

a) Prose (b) Poetry (c) Non-detail (d) Grammar and Writing

Three of the teachers said non-detail is easier to teach; grammar and poetry is easier to teach for two others, prose is easier for another and poetry for one.

3. Which are difficult and uninteresting to teach?

a) Prose (b) Poetry (c) Non-detail (d) Grammar and writing

For majority (5 nos.) of teachers, grammar and writing skill is difficult to teach to tribal learners. Prose and poetry is difficult for another two.

4. What is the difference between a prose piece and a poem?

   According to the teachers, the difference between prose and poetry is that there is no definite form in prose whereas poetry has a definite form and structure. The theme of prose is general and easier to teach whereas the theme of the poetry is difficult and confusing. Prose is informative whereas poetry is thought provoking and creative.

5. How is teaching of poetry different from teaching of prose?

   So far teaching is concerned; all the teachers said that teaching of prose is easier than teaching of poetry to tribal learners.

6. What according to you are the objectives of teaching poems?

   Some of them said that the main objective of teaching poetry is to enable the learners to imagine, create and enjoy.

7. Which subject do you prefer to teach personally?

   (a) Prose (b) Poetry

   In the opinion of the teachers, four of them like teaching of prose and three like teaching poetry.

8. What methods of teaching, according to you, are best suited for tribal learners?

   (a) Direct method (b) Grammar-translation Method (C) Structural Method

   (d) Other Four out of seven teachers said that Grammar-translation method is easier to teach the tribal students, where as one supported direct method and another opined for structural approach method. The methods should be interactive and learner-centred.

9. Why do you think so?

They believe that Grammar-translation method is easier both for teachers and tribal learners as well. It involves teaching through mother tongue. Structural method helps them to learn the structures and grammar. Direct method will help them to learn the language quickly.

10. Rate the poems that you have taught:

    a) Stopping by Woods on a Snowy Evening

    1. Difficult 2.Easy 3.Old 4.Boring 5.Interesting

    b) Oft, In the Stilly Night

    1. Difficult 2.Easy 3.Old 4.Boring 5.Interesting

    c) The Inchcape Rock

    1. Difficult 2.Easy 3.Old 4.Boring 5.Interesting

    d) To My True Friend

    1. Difficult 2.Easy 3.Old 4.Boring 5.Interesting

    e) Fishing

    1. Difficult 2.Easy 3.Old 4.Boring 5.Interesting

As stated by the teachers, all the poems are easy and interesting.

11. If difficult, why do you think difficult?

    (a).Words difficult (b). Theme is difficult (c). Very long

    The teachers opined that the poems are difficult for the tribal learners as they are too long and hence at times, boring.

12. If easy, why do you think easy?

    (a). Simple language (b). Interesting theme (c). Short poem

    The poems which are easy and interesting are so because of its simple and easy language and interesting theme.

13. From the poems taught by you, how much do you think the learners understand on their own without your help?

(a). Only 5% (b). 10% to 20% (c).30% to 40% (d). 50% to 70%

Four teachers believe that without the help of the teachers, the tribal learners can understand only 5% to 10%, whereas three teachers believe that they can understand 30 % to 40%.

14. Do you feel there are a good number of students in your class whose English language is much below their level? If yes, what is their rough percentage in the class?

All the teachers answered in affirmative. The detail is as follows:

Percentage	Teacher's Opinion
30% to 40%	15%
Above 50%	15%
Above 60%	15%
Abovc 70%	15%
Above 80%	43%

15. What are the probable reasons, according to you, for their weak performance in English?

Given below are some of the probable reasons, stated by the teachers which are the main cause of weak performance of the tribal students.

- Lack of vocabulary
- Lack of knowledge on tense, aspect and time
- Lack of proficiency in writing
- Fear for English
- Different cultural background
- Difference in mother tongue

- Socio-economic background
- Lack of creativity
- English as third or fourth language
- Less cared for in primary classes
- De-motivation to learn English

16. How do you judge that the students have understood the poem after your teaching in the class?

    They judge the student's learning by asking questions.

17. Which is better to teach language to tribal learners?

    (a). Prose (b). Poetry

    50% of the teachers opted for prose and 50% for poetry.

18. Whether poetry should be removed from their syllabus? Why?

    None of the teachers want poetry to be removed from their syllabus as it helps the students to enhance their creativity and imagination.

Teaching Poetry

1. What steps do you take to teach the poem?

    a) introduce the poem in an interesting way

    b) read aloud the poem

    c) ask them to read the poem silently for some time

    d) ask them questions from the poem

    e) give them interesting tasks/ activities from the poem

    f) ask them to do the activities in pair/ group?

    Majority (80%) of the teachers do all the above mentioned activities in teaching in class.

2. Do you explain through giving a lecture on the poem and explaining the meaning of the difficult words? (Yes/No)

   70% of the teachers explain through giving lecture on the poem and explaining the meaning of the difficult words.

3. While teaching do you move around the class or just stay near the board and explain/ lecture?

   (a). move around the class (b) just stay near the board and explain/ lecture

   All the teachers move around the class while teaching.

4. Do you use the blackboard? If yes, to what purpose?

   The teachers use the blackboard to do various activities like meaning, explaining through pictures, etc.

5. What according to you are the traits that a good teacher must possess?

   One who teaches in simple and interesting ways and allows students to understand it on their own with little help when necessary

   or

   One who selects difficult poems and only explains the poem through lectures without allowing the students to understand on their own.

   All the teachers believe that one who teaches in simple and interesting ways and allow students to understand it on their own with little help when necessary is actually a good teacher.

6. Do you give some writing tasks on poems and provide them with feedback?

   (Yes / No)

   All the teachers answered in affirmative.

7. Do you point out their errors and provide them suggestions to improve their English?

   (Yes / No)

   All the teachers answered in affirmative.

8. Have you ever tried to explain the poems using your own methodology and questions other than what has been provided in the text?

   (Yes / No)

   All the teachers answered in affirmative.

9. What modifications would you suggest in the present poetry syllabus to make it suitable for tribal learners?

   The teachers opinion regarding modifications in poetry syllabus are as follows:

   a) Poems should be short and simple

   b) It should be based on tribal culture and theme

   c) There should be more learner centered interesting activities in the syllabus

10. Do you think the poems taught to them are difficult for those low-proficient learners? If yes, how do you help them?

    a) Yes, they are difficult. But repeated discussions help.

    b) Yes. I help them by giving them other poems which suit their level.

    c) Yes, explain them in the class, give notes, respond to their questions during or after lectures.

    d) By interpreting the lines at the immediate constituent level/ word level

e) Yes. Take pains to explain the poems in the simplest possible language which are within their level of comprehension.

f) Make them read the stanzas many times. Ask them lead questions so that they are led to understand the content.

g) Not difficult.

As per the opinion of the teachers,

- The poems which are taught to the tribal students are difficult but repeated discussions help them.
- The poems should be selected carefully to suit their level.
- They help them in the class by giving notes, responding to their questions during or after lectures.
- Interpreting the lines at the immediate constituent level/word level also matters.
- Explaining the poems in the simplest possible way.

11. What are the suggestions for helping them to learn in your poetry class?

a) Select poems which suit their level; Select poems which can profitably be used to teach them English language; Design learner-friendly tasks from the poem

b) Reading aloud the poem in group, doing activities

c) Make them read and enjoy poetry free from conditions imposed by examination; ask them right questions to simulate interest in various aspects of poetry

d) By group activities, they should make friendship with like-minded persons and 'each one teach one' principle should be followed by them. I will supervise their activities.

e) Force them to participate in the process of learning by promoting activities. Teacher talks less and students do more activities.

f) Selection of good poems is of crucial importance. Then motivating the students to understand the beauty and value of the experience contained in the poems is also very important.

g) Motivation and repeated reading

h) Suggest for reading more

- 30% teachers suggested for all the options to help the students learn poetry in the class.
- 43% teachers suggested that the poems should suit the level of the learners so that it can profitably be used to teach them English language.
- 27% suggested for the selection of good poems is of utmost importance. Motivation to students is very much necessary to help the tribal learners learn English.

12. Should they be taught in their own language?

(Yes / No)

57% suggested against teaching them in their own language.

13. While teaching, do you stick to teacher's place or move around the class?

a) Both-more moving around

b) move around

c) stick to teacher's place

d) as per the situation in the class

e) all the time move around to promote involvement in the activities

f) sometimes I do move around the class if the class is not very large and if the classroom is not very congested

All of them stated that they move around in the class as per the requirement in the class.

14. Given below are some ways of teaching poems. Tick as many as you agree?

a) Introduce the poem

b) Provide pre-reading activities

c) ReaSd aloud the poem

d) Read aloud and then explain

e) Allow students to read silently

f) Ask questions to the students from the poem

g) While asking, advise the students to close the handouts/ books

h) Provide tasks/ activities on the poem

All the teachers provided different opinion regarding their ways of teaching.

- Teacher 1 – She normally does all the activities except advising the students to close their books. She also doesn't provide tasks or activities to students after/ before or while teaching.

- Teacher 2 – He does all the above mentioned activities but does not read aloud the poem before explaining.

- Teacher 3 – She does all the activities except providing tasks or activities to students after/ before or while teaching.

- Teacher 4 – He does all the above activities but doesn't read the poem aloud and ask the students to close their books or handouts while reading.

- Teacher 5 – She does all the above mentioned activities but does not read aloud the poem before explaining.
- Teacher 6 – She does all the activities except giving a formal introduction to the poem.
- Teacher 7 – She does all the above activities except reading aloud twice.

15. How do you test the students? Tick as many as you really do.

    a) Set long answer type questions

    b) Set short answer type questions

    c) Both a & b

    d) Set explanations from the poems taught

    e) Provide a poem not in the course and ask comprehension questions from the poem

    f) Provide feedback to the students on their performance

    All the teachers provided different opinion regarding their ways of teaching.

    - Teacher 1 – She normally sets both short and long type questions and set explanations from the poem taught.
    - Teacher 2 – He asks short questions to check whether the students have understood.
    - Teacher 3, 4 – She does all the activities mentioned so as to check their understanding.
    - Teacher 5,6 – They do all the above activities but doesn't give feedback to the students on their performance.
    - Teacher 7 – She does all the above mentioned activities except giving an unknown poem for explanation.

16. Do you think your students enjoy poems in English?

a) Yes, provided poems are not old and difficult. – but suits their level and are interesting for them (not for me)

b) Yes

c) Yes, they always do

d) This question is irrelevant to me. Students should be asked this question. But I hope they do enjoy, their feedback proves it.

e) No doubt about it

f) Yes, they do. As I stated above, much depends on the selection of the poems by the teacher and then drawing the attention of the students to the beauty and value of the poetic experience which, though subjective in a sense, is of universal nature.

g) Definitely, yes.

h) 43% teachers said that students enjoy the poems when they are not old and archaic, suits their level and are interesting to them. 14% said there is no doubt about it. Another 43% said that they enjoy the poems when it suits their level for which the selection of poem should be done meticulously keeping their understanding and background in mind.

From the responses of both of the questionnaires and the observation of classes as well as experience as a student, the researcher found that there are contradictions between the responses of both the teachers and the students. It is obvious that most of the students do not enjoy studying poetry. The teachers, on the other hand, do not try to find out what students need and what they find interesting. In most of the classes lecture, talk much and the students passively receive and talk less. Students who enjoy literature and poetry do not exceed 20% of the total percentage; most of them, from 80-90% usually mentally switch-off on use classes. It is worth here to quote from Dr.Kundu (1990) that: *This, of course has created a feeling of uneasiness and uncomfortability in the students and they tend to mentally switch off; the survival strategies of most of the present day learners in the classroom is mental switch-off. Most of the learners have no freedom to leave the classroom however uncomfortable and boring the classes might be. As they cannot absent themselves physically, they mentally switch off without giving us even a faint sign that they have switched off.*

The following table illustrates the difference between the responses of both teachers and students.

Table No. 4.1 The difference between the responses of both teachers and students

Students' Questionnaire	Teachers' Questionnaire
1. Only 9% students find poetry easy and 14% find it interesting.	Most of the teachers declare that the majority of the tribal learner that they teach are below the understanding level of their class. Besides they all admit that the poems which are taught to them are somehow difficult and they do their best to help them learn by repeated reading, explaining, activities, etc.
2. All the students at KISS are from tribal community.	None of the teachers belong to tribal community and hence has less awareness about tribal culture and background. None have received any special training in teaching to tribal students. They even have fixed notions regarding tribal people, their background and culture.
3.Approximately 70% of the students said that they like prose and not poetry.	Similarly, the teachers also feel that it is difficult to teach poetry to tribal learners than teaching of prose which is comparatively easier.
4. Almost 90% of the students rated the poems prescribed for them as difficult and boring.	But for the teachers, the poems are easier and interesting for tribal; learners.

Students' Questionnaire	Teachers' Questionnaire
5. The students consider the poems as difficult because of difficult words used in it, theme is not clearly understood by them.	`The teachers feel that the poems which are difficult for the students are long and boring.
6. In answering how much they can understand on their own without the teacher's help, the student's response ranges from 5% to 20%.	The teachers feel that students can understand 5% to 40% without their help.
7. The steps taken to teach the poems are the same as opted by both the students and teachers.	
8. The students want to be tested through short answer type questions.	The teachers response range from short answer type to long answer type, explanations of new poems etc.
	All the teachers believe that the poems prescribed for them are difficult. So the selection of the poem should be very careful. They should be taught poems which will be appropriate to their cultural background, suit their level of understanding and short in length.
Both the teachers and students want poetry to be a part of their syllabus.	

With the co-operation and consent of some of the Faculty members, the Researcher observed some of the poetry classes at KISS. The details of the class, teacher a, poem taught etc. are detailed below.

Class: 1st year H.S Science

Sec: A

Strength: 128

Present: 119

Period: 2nd Duration-1 hour Teacher's

Name: Mrs Kadambini Routray

Name of the Poem – Stopping By The Woods on a Snowy Evening

Poet-Robert Frost

As the class started, the teacher took attendance of the students and then told them to open their books. She started by asking some questions related to forest. She then told the poem which she was going to teach, wrote its name on the blackboard. She instructed the students to follow their books while she read it aloud. After completing the reading of the poem, she started to explain it line by line. While explaining, she wrote the meanings of the difficult words on the blackboard. As it was not a very long poem, the explanation got over quickly. Then she just asked the students some questions. The bell rang and she had to leave the class.

The researcher's observations during the entire class are:

- The introductory questions that the teacher asked could have been more interesting had she drawn the picture of a forest or shown them some pictures.
- The teacher read aloud the poem herself but didn't allow the students to read the poem loudly or even silently.
- The students were found to lose interest after 15/20 minutes and seemed to switch off mentally. The teacher didn't ensure whether the students are listening to her teaching.
- The words that she wrote were those that she felt difficult for the students. The students didn't ask any doubts.
- The questions that were asked at the end of the class, were responded to by only 4/5 students who seemed to be above average learners.

- She moved a bit while reading and explaining the poem. Her voice was audible to the last bench but she was not able to hold the attention of the students for long.
- The language of communication and explanation was mostly Odia.

Class: 1st year H.S Commerce

Sec: B

Strength: 128

Present: 123

Period: 2nd

Duration: 1 hour

Teacher's Name: Mr Haraprasad Mohapatra

Name of the Poem-Fishing

Poet-Gopa Ranjan Mishra

As the class started, the teacher took attendance of the students and then told them to open their books. He started by asking some questions related to their hobby. He also asked them whether they have gone fishing in their villages. He then wrote the name of the poem which he was going to teach on the blackboard. He instructed the students to close their books and listen to him while he read the poem. Then he instructed them to follow their books while he read it aloud again. After completing the reading of the poem, he started to explain it line by line. While explaining, he wrote the meanings of the difficult words on the blackboard. As it is a long poem, the explanation didn't get over completely. Then he asked the students some questions. The bell rang and he had to leave the class. The poem would be completed the next class.

The researcher's observations during the entire class are:

- The introductory questions that the teacher asked were interesting as he was able to draw the attention of the students to the poem.
- The teacher read aloud the poem himself and allowed the students to read the poem twice.
- The students were found to show interest in the poem.
- The words that he wrote were those that he felt difficult for the students. The students didn't ask any doubts.
- The questions that were asked at the end of the class, were responded to by only 4/5 students who seemed to be above average learners.
- He moved a bit while reading and explaining the poem. His voice was audible to the last bench and he was able to hold the attention of the students for long.
- The language of communication and explanation was mostly Odia and sometimes English.

Class: 1st year H.SCommerce

Sec: B

Strength: 128

Present: 123

Period: 2nd

Duration: 1 hour

Teacher's Name: Mr Trailokyanath Parida

Name of the Poem – To My True Friend

Poet-Elizabeth Pinard

As the class started, the teacher took attendance of the students and then told them to open their books. He started by asking some questions related to their hobby. He also asked them whether they have gone fishing in their villages. He then wrote the name of the poem which he was going to teach on the blackboard. He instructed the students to close their books and listen to him while he read the poem. Then he instructed them to follow their books while he read it aloud again. After completing the reading of the poem, he started to explain it line by line. While explaining, he wrote the meanings of the difficult words on the blackboard. As it is a long poem, the explanation didn't get over completely. Then he asked the students some questions. The bell rang and he had to leave the class. The poem would be completed the next class.

The researcher's observations during the entire class are:

- The introductory questions that the teacher asked were interesting as he was able to draw the attention of the students to the poem.
- The teacher read aloud the poem himself and allowed the students to read the poem twice.
- The students were found to show interest in the poem.
- The words that he wrote were those that he felt difficult for the students. The students didn't ask any doubts.
- The questions that were asked at the end of the class, were responded to by only 4/5 students who seemed to be above average learners.
- He moved a bit while reading and explaining the poem. His voice was audible to the last bench and he was able to hold the attention of the students for long.
- The language of communication and explanation was mostly Odia and sometimes English.

Class: 1st year H.S Arts

Sec: D

Strength: 128

Present: 123

Period: 2nd

Duration: 1 hour

Teacher's Name: Mrs Bedamati Pattnaik

Name of the Poem – The Inchcape Rock

Poet-Robert Southey

As the class started, the teacher took attendance of the students. Then she wrote words like sea, pirate, holy man and bell on the blackboard and asked the students to think and say what comes to their mind. The students got interested, though their response was not that encouraging. She then told a short story depicting the moral "As you sow, so shall you reap" in Odia. Thereafter, she wrote the name of the poem which she was going to teach on the blackboard. She instructed the students to close their books and listen to her while she read the poem. Then she instructed them to follow their books while she read it aloud again. Thereafter, she told them to close their eyes and think the poem what they have understood in their mind. She even asked them to say the words that they have remembered while listening to the poem twice. After that she started to explain the poem line by line. While explaining, she wrote the meanings of the difficult words on the blackboard both in Odia and English. As it is a long poem, the explanation didn't get over completely. She could complete only the first section of the poem. She asked the students some questions to answer orally and one question was given to write on the blackboard. The bell rang and she had to leave the class. The poem would be completed the next class.

The researcher's observations during the entire class are:

- The introductory activities that the teacher undertook were interesting as she was able to draw the attention of the students to the poem.

- The teacher read aloud the poem herself and allowed the students to read the poem twice. She also told them to have a mental picture of the entire poem.
- By asking them to say the words that they remember, she could make every student attentive and alert.
- The students were found to show interest in the poem.
- The words that she wrote were those that she felt difficult for the students. The students didn't ask any doubts. She wrote the meanings both in Odia and English which helped to clarify their concept and meaning of the words.
- The questions that were asked at the end of the class, were responded to by only 40% of the students.
- She moved a bit while reading and explaining the poem. Her voice was audible to the last bench and she was able to hold the attention of the students for long.
- The language of communication and explanation was mostly Odia and sometimes English.

From the above observations, it is evident that the teacher who had involved the students in the teaching process, is actually a good teacher as she was able to do justice to imparting teaching. But the other teachers who were only lecturing were actually seemed to be doing their duty of teaching where the students were only passive learners...switched off mentally.

5

Preparation of Materials

The present Chapter is all about the preparation of materials-An Anthology of Poems for the tribal students.

Materials, in a broader sense, are anything used to help learners learn. In case of ELT, these mainly include textbooks, supplementary readers, real objects, picture, maps, charts, diagrams, tape recorders, radio, TV, computer, etc. In countries like India, materials mainly mean textbooks. The textbooks play an important role in English Language Teaching (ELT) where teaching/learning is mainly examination-oriented.

Materials, to start with, in the past, were restricted to oral literatures such as folk-tales, folk songs and riddles. When the British came to India, they felt difficulty in communicating with the Indians who had no common link language with them. Hence, they felt that if they could not communicate, it would be difficult to rule the nation. In order to find a solution, they searched for a group of Indians who could act as a medium to communicate with the mass. So, the Indians who could communicate with the Britishers emerged as the new elite class of Indian society. Later when the Christian missionaries came to India, they started establishing primary schools where the medium of instruction was the local language. Thereafter they started establishing high schools where the medium of instruction was English. As the medium of instruction in universities in India established by the British was English, the demand for an education in English from school level started gaining momentum. In this mission to teach English to

Indian in order to create a mass of people who would be," Indian in looks but British in thought and opinion", printing press at Serampore had played a pivotal role. The press published bibles in the local language and people started to get access to western thought and religion. Thus English as a language started gaining a lot of importance in Indian society.

After the coming of prints, books of literature such as dramas, poems, stories, essays and novels were written. Latin was the first language to be formally taught. At the end of the 19th century a series of experiments were conducted in the area of textbook writing and the focus shifted from teaching of Latin to teaching of English. In 1960s there were quick and massive developments in most of the foundation disciplines, more particularly for language teaching, in linguistics and psychology. All these brought about a sea-change in the preparation of textbooks.

Teaching/learning situation in India is very different from that of Western countries. This is very true of ELT, more particularly with regard to ELT materials.

In Western rich countries English is taught in comfortable circumstances. The small size of their class (only 20 students in a class), rich infrastructure (good building, classroom, modern equipment, furniture, etc.) and teaching of English as mother tongue add to their comfort. But in India English is taught in very difficult circumstances. Large class size (60-100 students in a class), poor infrastructure and teaching of English as a second or foreign language add to the difficulties. Besides, the learners are low-proficient in English. Teachers' (school teachers, in particular) proficiency in the language is also low. They too lack proper training in ELT. The education system is more examination oriented. Students study only for examination. There is little exposure to English outside the classroom.

Textbooks can broadly be divided into three major types; course book, anthology or a mixed type (courses + anthology). Course books are mostly written by the textbook writers themselves keeping in view a particular group of students. Course books are more suitable for the beginners. But in Western countries they are also used for higher classes. Anthologies are collection of writings of creative writers (poets, short stories writers, novelists, playwrights). The textbook writers only select these creative writings to suit the level of the learners. They add necessary notes and glossing, comprehension questions, exercises and activities. Anthologies are good for learners of higher levels such as in college. In India, anthologies are more in use (but often carelessly prepared) because English courses in higher classes are more literature oriented. Besides, they are not prepared by English language teaching experts alone. Just a short biography on the poet or the writer precedes the poem or the text which is in most cases not followed by questions, activities or exercises.

Approximately 25% of India's population is constituted of tribal people. Moreover, the rest of the population consists of approximately 50% poor and lower middle class. So, when we frame a syllabus keeping in mind the middle class and upper middle class students (as is the case in the present context), it is quite obvious that more than 50% of the students will find it alien to their livid realities.

We have observed that the existing English text books are based on urban middle class values and create cultural problems for tribal learners. This is also instrumental in creating in them, a negative attitude to their own culture. Thus while preparing text books for them attempts should be made to reduce this cultural gap. When the cultural differences are slight, the teacher's explanation will help tribal pupils in understanding the cultural content. But when the difference is great, the teacher's explanation is not very useful or effective. Wherever possible, the material should also try to foster in them a love for their own culture. While preparing text books in English the following points can be taken into consideration. (These points can be more strictly followed while preparing reading materials in tribal languages and the 'languages of their early experience'.)

The entry behaviour of the tribal learners should be taken into consideration and the initial learning materials should be geared to their existing state of readiness.

The vocabulary, structures and the cultural content of the materials should be carefully graded facilitating efficient sequential learning.

The materials should have high interest value for tribal learner. This can be done by including subjects which are close to their experience and environment. Rapid Readers should be based on realistic stories featuring exciting adventures. These Readers and stories should be short and more in number. This will give them a sense of accomplishment in having read more books in a short time. As the majority of tribal students come from working class families whose long term goals are seldom sought, this will give them the pleasure of accomplishment at the earliest possible moment.

The subject-matter should be such as to foster in them a sense of love and pride in their language and culture. This can be done by including topics on their culture local traditions, festivals, folk-lore, history, music, art and biography of important tribals. Preparing materials on such topics for tribes like the Santal will not be very difficult as much has been written on them, their customs, traditions, religion and folk tales.

The materials should be carefully selected for educational, social and moral values. Subjects which aggravate their fear of the invisible world, support beliefs in witchcraft and superstitions should be avoided. This does not mean that the subjects should be used as a basis for moralizing, but rather they should furnish worthwhile content for education as well as language pedagogy.

The tribals are highly musical people and have great love for songs and riddles. Some of their folk-songs, therefore, can be translated into English (already many of them are available in English) and prescribed for teaching purposes. Poems based on riddles, of musical value, can also be used effectively.

6

Try Outs and Findings

This chapter, the sixth one, is about tryout of the materials suggested and the findings.

The class, the location and the time

The study, as stated before, is confined to first year of Higher Secondary class, Kalinga Institute of Social Sciences (KISS), Bhubaneswar. Ideally, therefore, the material should have been tried out in the poetry class of plus two first year class. This was not possible as the students are to study their prescribed poetry course in their poetry classes. So we had to find out other ways of trying the material out on these students. With the help of the Principal and colleagues, we arranged a class of about 100 students of plus two first year class who volunteered for the try out class every day for two weeks after their regular classes. As KISS is a fully residential institution, it was quite easier to arrange the classes. Thus we got about two hours every day in the first two weeks of January 2016. We got about 18 hours to tryout the material. The classes took place in the college between 3:30 to 5:30.

Arranging the class for a Learner-centred Approach

Large classes are unsuitable for language learning through literature approach. It needs learner-centered classes. Small and learner-centered classes are good for language teaching. But our large classes make this almost impossible. We, therefore, had to arrange the classroom to suit language through literature approach. We divided the class into four subsections by making two roads, one vertical and the other horizontal as shown below:

Table No. 6.1 Pattern of Arrangement of Benches in Class

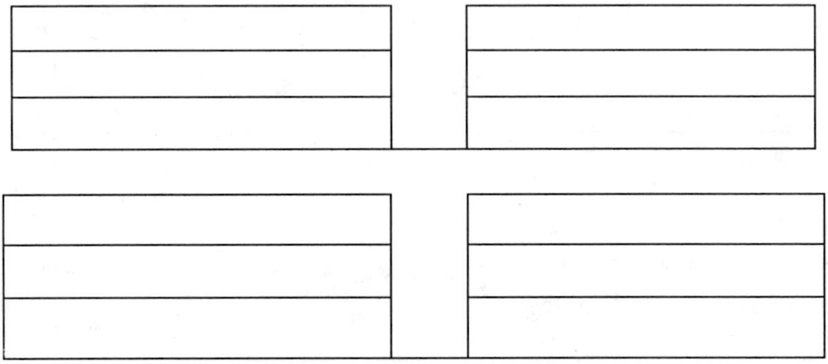

The class time was divided between small teacher talks (about 10-15%) and the rest time for the students to work with the tasks provided to them in the form of worksheets. When the teacher has to give instructions, s/he comes to the teacher's place, or else s/he is to be with the students moving along the two roads created to watch students doing the task and helping them individually when they need his/her help. The teacher, because of the roads, can easily move inside the class and can see from very close quarters the students doing the task. The material provided included the poem along with the questions and activities to be done in workbook format in the workbook itself.

Steps/Methods of Teaching Followed

The following steps/ methods are generally followed to handle the poems in the classroom:

1. Introduction:

   The poem was introduced mainly through the pre-reading activity suggested at the beginning of each poem. At times pictures and photographs are also used, the main purpose being motivating the learners to read the poem.

2. Reading aloud the poem

The poem was read aloud twice, first, students only listened to the poem read aloud by the teacher and second, students listen to the teacher reading aloud at the same time looking at the printed poem.

3. Silent reading of the poem by the students

   The students were asked to read the poem silently. The teacher moved inside the class to ensure that they were engaged in reading.

4. Comprehension and appreciation questions by the teacher from the poem

   First, comprehension questions were asked generally beginning with global questions (what was the poem about; who were there in the poem, etc.). Second, appreciation questions were asked. These questions were mostly based on the questions provided in the lesson. The following classroom questioning skills are made use of at this stage:

   - ask appropriate question to the appropriate student;
   - a phrase or an incomplete sentence could be enough; full sentence is not necessary for low-proficient learners;
   - provided feedback to the students for answering a question or even a part of the question.
   - do not concentrate on the clever students, get everyone involved in questions and answers;
   - ask a question to the whole class, give the students sometime to think and then ask individual students to answer the question. *(Based on Dr. Kundu's class notes).*

   Attempt is made to exploit the poem fully through asking as many questions to as many students possible.

5. Answering the comprehension questions in the workbook

Here students were told that they could get part of the answer from the question itself and part from the poem. Here they were taught to write correct sentences based on the factual understanding of the poem.

6. Answering appreciation questions

   At this stage, students were allowed to think critically and were given some freedom to answer the questions in their own way. They were allowed to use more than one sentence, even at times a paragraph, where necessary.

7. Doing the activities

   At this stage students were often allowed to do the task in pairs and group where possible. Some of the task/activities which could not be done in the class were given as home task.

   In steps 1, 2 and 4, the teacher occupied the teacher's place, most of the time as s/he had to address to whole class. But in steps 3, 5, 6 and 7 s/he was in the learner's space moving inside the class watching students doing their tasks in the workbook and helping individually who needed help. If there was any doubt or if the instructions for some tasks are not clear for many of the students, s/he cames to occupy the teacher's place to address the whole class or to use the blackboard to clarify the point.

Some of the major findings of the tryout are stated below

1. Most of the students are able to comprehend and enjoy the poems on their own with minimum help from the teacher as the poems are simple, interesting and graded from simple to slightly difficult ones. The first three poems Mice, What Do You Plant? and Springtime are very easy. This was, as stated before, done deliberately as starters to change the attitude of the students. By being exposed to old and difficult poems and the only method of learning through explanation of each line of the poem by the teacher, the

students have developed the wrong attitude to poem – that they cannot comprehend poems on their own unless explained to them in detail by the teacher. This is what a student wrote when we asked their opinions about some of the poems:

> The poem was nice because the word which the poet cesed was eazy. , the described things which the most people know it. I liked this poem because it was easy and clear. I mean when i read any poem and understard i liked. But when i face difficult poem then i have the poetry in general.

2. To start with, most of the students, excepting a few whose English is good, had problem even answering one sentence answer questions from the poem (How have you understood the poem?) which are the easiest. And we have, as stated before, provided them with tips how to answer them correctly getting part of the answer from the question and part from the poem. But instead of taking our tips, many of them went on answering in their own way and went wrong. We, therefore, had to tell them repeatedly the tips to help them come up with correct sentences. Only towards the third poem they were able to set them right.

> Mice
>
> - What does the poet think about the mice ?
>
> Ans – The poet think about the mice ~~are~~ nic .
>
> 2. What are the tals of mice like?
>
> A – The tals of mice alike long .
>
> 3 What ar there face lik ?
>
> A – There fac like smal .

3. Most of the students had problems in answering the appreciation questions. Here they have to think critically and use their mind to infer the answer as, unlike the factual questions in the previous section, these questions are difficult. Most of the students have problem here as the traditional method of teaching poems – explaining everything to them and asking them only long answer-type, often predictable questions – had developed in them the wrong habit of memorizing the answers without (or with little) understanding. Fortunately, as we progressed with our lessons, most of them learned to think and apply their mind to get right answers to these appreciation questions.

Childhood

1.Q. What does the poe want to know?

Ans. The poet wants to know when did his childhoo go.

2.Q. What did he realise about Hell and Haven?

He realised about Hel and Haven that they could not be fund in geography book.

4. Most of the students liked the activities / tasks though initially they had problems to do them as they were not exposed to this kind of task before. It is worth quoting a student's opinion in this regard:

The best question is Q.3(b). At First I hate the question becouse I have ~~thing~~ think that I can never write a poem or even silly poem, but I started to write, I Felt very interesting. really I Feel jealous of the Poets, because they ~~aly~~ always Feel this interesting. It was the difficult and the best one.

He refers here to the types of tasks which encouraged them to write poems. The task in question was: "The poet wrote the poem in support of mice. But you don't like mice. Can you write a poem against mice following the pattern of the poem. The first two lines are given for you":

"I think mice

Are not nice"

{They like living in dark place

Running here and there

Making troubles everywhere

Girls and children always fear}.

} Done by a student

5. Helping the learners learn language through literature involves changing the old mindset of the students and also changing the wrong strategies of learning they have developed due to wrong materials and method of teaching. Some of the wrong strategies, which, the use of the materials and methods attempted to change, are as follows:

a.

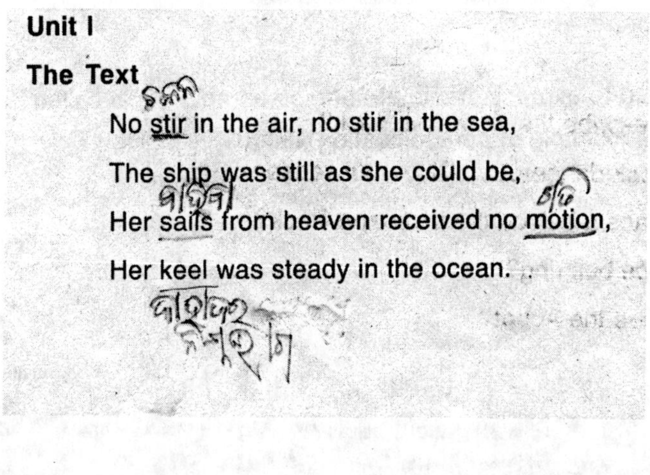

Unit I

The Text

No stir in the air, no stir in the sea,

The ship was still as she could be,

Her sails from heaven received no motion,

Her keel was steady in the ocean.

Students are found to consult immediately a pocket dictionary to get the meanings of new or difficult words they come across in a poem without trying to guess the meaning from the context. This wrong strategy is due to exposure to difficult poems with archaic words in which getting the meanings of new words seems to be the most important, or at times, the only task they are supposed to do. But we encouraged the learners to guess the meaning from the context. Learners had initial problems to do this. The poem *The Inchcape Rock*, has some difficult words. The learners are found to immediately consult their dictionaries and write the meanings on the poem.

THE INCHCAPE ROCK 107

Without either sign or sound of their shock
The waves flowed over the Inchcape Rock;
So little they rose, so little they fell,
They did not move the Inchcape Bell.

The Abbot of Aberbrothok
Had placed that bell on the Inchcape Rock;
On a buoy in the storm it floated and swung,
And over the waves its warning rung.

When the Rock was hid by the surge's swell,
The mariners heard the warning bell;
And then they knew the perilous Rock,
And blessed the Abbot of Aberbrothok.

Glossary

keel	bottom part of the ship
buoy	a floating object on the sea to mark a dangerous place
surge's swell	rise of the tidal waves
mariner	sailor

Think it out

1. How does the poet describe the Inchcape Rock?
2. Was the Inchcape Rock dangerous? Give your reasons?
3. Why did the Abbot place a bell on the Inchcape Rock?
4. When did the Inchcape bell ring?
5. Why did mariners bless the Abbot?

The glossary and notes in the last pages, I think it will be better if it is written after the poem or don't write it at all.

We deliberately, as stated above, provided the glossary at the end of the unit, not after the poem. This student found it difficult to consult them at the end. She, therefore, comments:

a. After this observation we had to convince the learners the fact that it is possible to guess, at least partly, the meaning of a new word from the context provided they make an attempt in this regard. This worked but took time because of long use of wrong strategy.

b. While writing to answer questions or do the task, most of the learners initially tried to write without thinking. They wrote and cut it and then rewrote. Taking note of this fact, we suggested them to follow three steps of writing-Think, Write, Revise and then if necessary rewrite. This also worked but took time. The learners are not accustomed to go through these steps of writing as they mostly mug up what they want to write in the exam and there is no need to think to do this.

c. In reading, the learners are found to have many wrong strategies. The best strategy of reading is to skim quickly the whole text and then read it part by part in detail. Getting an overall idea helps one to understand the parts better. But the learners are found to have the wrong strategy of reading everything, part by part and then get the whole idea. They have also the wrong idea that to understand a text one has to understand the meaning of all the words of the text which is not true. We have really worked hard to change this attitude of learners with regard to reading.

I loved the activities. They are interesting and comprehensive. They are related to our daily life and that made me enjoy them. The poem is new for me. I think, if students are taught these poems and in good ways with similar activities they will love poetry.

Jobamani Soren

d. Initially, we came across the problem of many of the students copying answer from their friends whose English is better than theirs. To do this, they managed to sit by their side. Doing this, for long, they have become totally dependent on their friends, a kind of parasite, and have lost their self-confidence. We had to change their seats and rebuild their self-confidence asking them to do very simple tasks to begin with.

6. The home tasks given did not work as most of the students copied them from their better friends. We, therefore, had to stop giving home tasks and make them do the task in classes. We also had to convince them of the fact that if they copy from their friends they are not actually helping them learn English.

7. Most of the students did the tasks and improved their English. But still many are found not to be serious about the tasks and the course as these are not related to their exam. In Odisha, students are highly exam-oriented. They do not study anything not related to their exam. The course, therefore, would have worked better if made a part of their regular course with exam.

I enjoyed reading the poems especially when you look at the glossary at the end of the poem to get the meaning of difficult words. Reading become more enjoyable as you go further through the task, "activities and questions". As more you read more familiar you become with the poem, because these activities give you more chance to go through the poem and each time you discover things you read betweem the lines.

Ranjita Majhi.

8. Finally we realized from our tryout that it is very difficult to help the low-proficient learners learn English as we found that students with some proficiency in English gained more from the course than students with very low proficiency. Not only their proficiency is too low to get

benefit even out of the simplest material, but also they are convinced of the fact that the system cannot but pass them in spite of their very low proficiency.

To ascertain the fact that the tribal learners will learn English better if they are taught language through literature, the researcher observed a few of the prose classes as well.

The findings are as follows

1. The teacher, in introducing the prose (both prose and non-detail) piece used questions as the tool to introduce the topic. But the tribal students found uninteresting, dry and factual.
2. The lecture method of teaching of the prose pieces, non-flexibility, and lack of scope for experimentation, led the students to switch off mentally.
3. The teacher himself seemed quite uninterested and seemed to be teaching in the class as a routine work just to complete the syllabus.
4. The activities at the end of the lesson did not provide any scope for imagination and creativity for the students as well.
5. Overall, it was not at all a pleasurable experience both for the teacher and the student.

7

Conclusion

The following conclusions are drawn from the study which prove most of our pre-suppositions we started with, in Chapter One:

1. The language through literature approach is more useful in the context of teaching English to tribals than only literature approach.
2. The anthology we prepared will help learners not only improve their English, but also equip them with literary skills provided suitable methods of teaching are used.
3. Students neither learn language nor develop literary skills from a course of difficult English poems of English poets which is taught using a teacher-centred approach and tested through questions which promote memorization.
4. Only introducing an anthology of poems based on the principle of language through literature approach will not work unless the methods of teaching and evaluation change to suit the course. For example, the learner-centered approach is to be used to handle the material and instead of forcing the student to memorize answer to examination questions, the pattern of questions should be changed. Instead of basing the test on the poem taught, questions can be given from a poem not taught. But the poem should be simple and provided in the question paper. Similarly, instead of asking long answer-type questions (most of which can be predicted), task-like questions can be given with the original poem. As teaching/learning in Odisha is

highly exam-oriented and education means examination, and exam means marks, positive changes can be brought about only through positively changing the system of examination.

5. Finally, to conclude, our anthology helped students change their negative attitude to poetry developed through selection of old and difficult poems and through teaching them by explaining the poem. Stated below is the response of a girl to our anthology. This girl's English is good. She is not a low-proficient learner. But she volunteered for the class with some other learners who are not low-proficient. Her comment really shocked us. We had impression that at least the learners whose English is good enjoy the traditional poetry course. But this, as seen from her comment, is not the case:

> I enjoyed reading the poems especially when you look at the glossary at the end of the poem to get the meaning of difficult words. Reading become more enjoyable as you go further through the task, " activities and questions". As more you read more familiar you become with the poem, because these activities give you more chance to go through the poem and each time you discover things you read betweem the lines.
>
> Ramjita Majhi.

The suggested anthology will not only be extremely suitable and useful to tribal learners but also will cater to the needs of average and above average students. So it will serve the purpose of teaching language through literature to all the students specially focusing on the low-proficient tribal learners who actually need to be uplifted through language learning.

States with a substantial tribal population should establish autonomous Institutes of Tribal Languages to undertake research in tribal languages and dialect and publish books on tribal literature and language. The existing Tribal Welfare Institutes of Odisha should be given autonomous status to carry on independent research and survey and to objectively re-evaluate Government activities for the upliftment of tribals. The U.G.C which at present gives special financial help to colleges which have a good number of tribal students should also earmark some research fellowships for carrying on research on tribal language and literature.

In devising and selecting methods for teaching English to tribal students, their learning styles should be taken into consideration. *The tribals lay more stress on learning by memory. Due to lack of scripts they have a deeply entrenched oral tradition. Everything is orally recorded in their memories and handed down from generation to generation. Most of the things they want to remember are put in the form of songs, as the music, rhythm and repetition act as aids to memory. For instance, in order to memorize easily and quickly the great number of different rhymes, the Santals have invented a series of mnemonics which they repeat at the opening of a dance or song* (Culshaw, 1949). The tribals are also very fond of riddles and storytelling. Learning, for them, is an active pleasurable event, mostly carried on with peers. Based on this oral reading, recitation, repetition, group methods, role-playing and story-telling may profitably be applied in teaching English to tribal pupils. As learning is a pleasurable event with the tribals, every attempt should be made to make the method interesting by use of a variety of teaching techniques in a variety of learning contexts.

Analysis of the question papers in English tests are also largely geared to the urban middle class culture. The tribal pupils lack test-taking skills and have less motivation for taking tests than their middle class counterparts. What Douvan observes about I.Q. tests is also true of other tests. She observes: *In the area of motivation, it is clear that middle-class children are more motivated to do well on examinations of the I.Q. sort because of the general emphasis on success and competition in middle class life.* (1956: 220)

In a test for tribal pupils, therefore, the instructions should be very clear and the content should not create too many cultural problems for them. More practice in taking tests should be given as we know tribal pupils are slow and cautious in their approach and poor in the skills of reading. A series of 'formative' tests should be administered, so designed as to give them a sense of achievement at every stage and provide feedback to learn.

From the responses of the English teachers of tribal pupils to some of the items in the questionnaire and observation of some of their English lessons, it is apparent that they have little knowledge of tribal culture, negative attitudes to tribal culture and language and stereotypes of tribals. This necessitates additional training for them which the existing traditional training programmes do not provide. Further, the new role which the teaching of English is required to play as a part of multicultural education in pluralistic societies, requiring cooperation among teachers of English, teachers of other subjects and specialists in bilingual education, necessitates changes in the existing training programmes for English language teaching. Besides training in English language teaching, topics such as tribal linguistics, culture, community relations etc. should be included in a teacher-training programme for the English teachers of tribal pupils.

The researcher felt the dearth of valid information on the life styles of tribals and tribal pupils though there are numerous anthropological and sociological analyses of the major tribal communities. Researches, therefore, can be undertaken on their life styles, styles of learning and value systems. Contrastive studies of major tribal languages and major Indian languages (like Oriya and Santali) can also be undertaken to find out their problems in learning major regional languages.

Contrastive studies of English and major tribal languages can also be done, which will provide valuable information about their linguistic problems in learning English. Experiments can also be conducted with some of the methods of teaching like role-playing, recitation, group-work, story-telling to ascertain their effectiveness in teaching English to the tribal pupils. Similar research can also be undertaken for other major tribes.

Researches therefore can be undertaken on the lifestyle, styles of learning and value system of particular tribal communities; it can further extend to the teaching of language through prose or non-detailed stories. Contrastive studies can also be made on the effectiveness of teaching through their own language and the regional language also with English language. This will also provide valuable information regarding their linguistics problems and its elimination. Experiments can also be made on some of the methodologies of teaching like role-playing, recitation, group work, storytelling and their effectiveness. This study intends to help elevate the standard of learning of English of the tribal learners to a great extent.

Bibliography

A Model English Reader, Board of Secondary Education, 1995.

Adiseshiah. M. S and Ramanathan. S.. *(1974) Educational Problems of Scheduled Castes and Scheduled Tribes in Tamil Nadu,* Madras Institute of Developmental Studies.

Annual Report of Scheduled Castes and Scheduled Tribes Development, Minorities and Backward Classes Welfare Department, Government of Odisha. (2014-15)

Annual Report of the Commission for Scheduled Castes and Scheduled Tribes, 2014.

Annual Report, Women and Child Development Department, Odisha.

Arya, R.C, *The Question of Methodology in the Teaching of Literature*, CIEFL Bulletin, Vol. 13, 1977, No 1. Print.

Bannell, Ralph Ings, Rev of *Language Teaching Methodology: A Textbook for Teachers by David Nunan* P. ELT Journal, Vol. 49, Oct 1995, No.4. Print.

Basu, D.D. *The Constitution of India,* Professional Book Publishers; 2015 edition (2016)

Batstone, Rob, *Teachers and Course Design,* ELT Journal, Vol. 42, July 1988, No 3. Print.

Baurain, Bradley, *Small Group Multitasking in Literature Classes,* ELT Journal, Vol. 61, July 2007, No 3. Print.

Block, David, *Some Thoughts on DIY Materials Design,* ELT Journal, Vol 45, Jul 1991, No 3. Print.

Brumfit, C. J.(ed) (1983) *Teaching Literature Overseas: Language-Based Approaches'* ELT Documents 115, British Council, Pergamon Press.

Brumfit, C. J.(ed.) (1985) *Language and Literature Teaching: From Practice to Principle*, Pergamon.

Census Report, 2011, Government of Odisha.

Chaudhuri (ed.), *Education and Literacy Programmes,* Delhi: Mittal Publications.

Chitni. Suma.(1974). *The Educational Problems of Scheduled Caste and Tribe College students in Maharashtra,* TISS, Bombay.

Christison, M.A. (1982) *English Through Poetry*, Alemany Press.

Collie, J. and Slater, S. (1987) *Literature in the Language Classroom: A Resource Book on Ideas and Activities,* Cambridge University Press

Cotterall, Sara. *Promoting Learner Autonomy Through the Curriculum: Principles for Designing Language Courses Skills with EAP Classes,* ELT Journal, Vol 54, Apr 2000, No 2. Print.

Crammer, David, "Rev of The Inward Ear – Poetry in the Language Classroom by Alan Malley & Alan Duff", *P.ELT Journal*, Vol 46, Apr 1992, No.2. Print

Dasgupta, N.K. (1963): *Problems of Tribal Education and the Santals,* Bharatiya Adimjati Sevak Sangha, New Delhi.

Datta, Chitra, *English For Academic Purposes: Model For A Course-Design For Indian Learners*, Vol-3,1991, No1,2.

Demographic Details, Census of India, 2011, Government of Odisha.

Dissemination Workshop, *Status of Scheduled Castes and Scheduled Tribes in Orissa.*

Dubey.S.M. (1974). *Study of Scheduled Caste and Scheduled Tribe College Students in Assam, Department of Sociology*, Dibrugarh University.

Ezekiel, Nissim. *Collected Poems*, 2001.

George, P.T, *Bridging the Gap Between School and College – Report of a Try Out of the Stariway Reading Course*, CIEFL Bulletin, Vol. 13, 1977, No 1. Print.

George, P.T. *Teaching English to the Disadvantaged Sections of the Community – Towards the Development of a Curricular Strategy*, CIEFL Bulletin, Vol 18, 1982, No 1&2. Print.

Harbordl, John, *The Use of the Mother Tongue in the Classroom,* ELT Journal, Vol 46, Oct 1992, No 4. Print.

Harmer, J. *How to Teach English,* (Review), ELT Journal, Vol 62, July 2008, No 3. Print.

Hill, David. Rev of *How To Teach English by Jeremy Harmer* P. ELT Journal, Vol 54, Jul 2000, No. 3.Print.

Hirvela, Alan and Boyle, Joseph, *Literature Courses and Students Attitude,* ELT Journal, Vol 42, Jul 1988, No 3. Print.

Hornbill, National Council for Technical Education and Research, New Delhi, Jan 2013.

Kundu, M. 1980. *Teaching English to Tribal Learners: A Survey of the Ethnic, Cultural, Socio-Economic and Linguistic Problems involved,* With Some Suggestions For a Viable Pedagogy.

Kundu, M. 1990. *Tribal Education in India – Some Problem.* (pp.246-254), in: B.A Dissertation submitted at Central Institute of English and Foreign Language, Hyderabad.

.... *A Hand Book for Teachers of English,* ELT Move, Orissa, India. (1990)

.... *English Poems for Indian Children,* ELT Move, Orissa, Bhubaneswar. (1998).

.... *For Me, MS Institute of Rural ELT,* Jajpur, Orissa, India. (1998).

Kundu, Manmmatha. *The Journey From Literature to Teaching Language Through Literature: Are We Teachers of Literature Willing to Cross the Hurdles on the Way?* A Paper presented on the National Seminar on Teaching Language Through Literature: Problems and Principles 28-29 May 2006, Faculty of Arts, Sana'a University.

L.R.N. (1968) *Education and Modernization among the Munda and Oraon of Ranch,* Ph.D. Sociology, Patna University.

Lakra.S. (1976). *Impact of Education on the Tribals of Ranchi District,* Ph.D. Education, Patna University.

Lee, William R, Rev of *Advanced Communication Games by Jill Hadfield* P.ELT Journal, Vol 42, Apr 1988, No.2. Print.

Leech, G.N. (1969*) A Linguistic Guide to English Poetry,* Longman.

Lima, Chris. *ELT and the Challenges of the Time,* ELT Journal, Vol 63, July 2009, No 3. Print.

Lynch, Tony, *Questioning Roles in the Classroom,* ELT Journal, Vol 45, Jul 1993, No 3. Print.

Malley, Allan and Duff, Allan. *The Inward Ear: Poetry in the Language Classroom* (1992).

McKay, S. (1982) *'Literature in the ESL Classroom'*, *TESOL Quarterly*, Vol. 16, No.4, December 1982, pp. 529-36

Nadkarni, M.V. *English in Mother Tongue Medium Education*, Vol 19,1983, No.1. Print.

National Policy on Education, 1986

Nayar. P.K.B. (1975). *The Scheduled Caste and Tribe High School Students in Kerala,* Department of Sociology, Kerala University.

NUEPA.2009. *Elementary Education in India: Where Do We Stand?* State Report Cards 2007-08, National University of Educational Planning and Administration, New Delhi

NUEPA.2011. *Elementary Education in India: Where Do We Stand?* State Report Cards 2008-09, National University of Educational Planning and Administration, New Delhi

Orissa State Bureau of Textbook Preparation and Production, *Invitation to English-1,* Bhubaneswar, Orissa, India.2013-14.

Porte, Graeme, "Poor Language Learners and their Strategies for Dealing with New Vocabulary," *ELT Journal,* Vol 42, Jul 1988, No 3. Print.

Rao. M.L. (1976*) A Study of In-Group Out-Group Attitude Formation in Tribal and Non-Tribal Secondary School Children in Rajasthan*, Ph.D. Psychology, Udaipur University.

Rath.R. and Misra, S.K. (1974).*The Study of Scheduled Caste and Scheduled Tribe College Students in Orissa*, Department of Psychology, Utkal University.

Report of the Commission for Scheduled Castes and Scheduled Tribes, 2009, Government of India Report of the Education Commission, Government of India, (1972:70)

Report of the *Harijan* and *Adivasi* Commission, 1978-79

Report of the Secondary Education Commission, Government of India, (1972:70)

Report of the Study Group, 1964-66

Reviews

Richards, J.C. &Renandya, W. Rev of *Methodology in Language Teaching by Jeremy Harmer* P. ELT Journal, Vol 58, jan 2004, No.1, Print

Sachidananda.(1974). *Education among the Scheduled Castes and Scheduled Tribes in Bihar* (College Students), A.N.S. Institute of Social Studies, Patna.

Sastri, M.I, *Language and Effect in Poetry*, CIEFL Bulletin, Vol 13, 1972-73, No 9. Print.

Senior, Rose. *Class Centered Teaching*, ELT Journal, Vol 63,Oct 2009, No.4 Print.

Sharma, Devabrat. *Poems in Language Classroom,* A Paper presented on the National Seminar on Teaching Language Through Literature: Problems and Principles 28-29 May 2006, Faculty of Arts, Sana'a University.

Sheldon, *Leslie Rev of Materials and Methods in ELT: A Teacher's Guide* by Jo McDonough and Christopher Shaw P.ELT Journal, Vol 49, Oct 1995, No.4. Print

Tribal Profile at a Glance, May 2014

Tully, Mark, *English: An Advantage to India?,* ELT Journal, Vol 51, Apr 1997, No 2. Print.

Wedell, Martin. *Innovation in ELT*, ELT Journal, Vol 63, Oct 2009, No 4. Print.

Whispers of Immortality, Ed. Wilson, Anil. 2009

Appendix A
Students' Questionnaire

Dear Participants

It is my sincere request to you to fill this questionnaire so that I may get the data much needed for my study. The information collected will be used for research purpose only. I hope, your response will be of immense help for furtherance of my study in this direction.

Thank you.

Preetinanda Roy

Questionnaire for Students

Personal Data

1. Name: 2. Class/ Stream: 3. Sec: 4. Tribe: 5. District:

1. Do you have any tribal language of your own community?

   (a) Yes (b) No

2. **Is there any scripts available in that language?**

   (a) Yes (b) No

3. **In which language do you communicate at home earlier?**

   (a) Odia (b) Own tribal language

4. **In which language do you communicate at home now?**

   (a) Odia (b) Own tribal language

5. **If you have other language than Odia, at what age did you start learning the following languages?**

   (a) Tribal Language------- yrs

   (b) Odia--------------------- yrs

   (c) Hindi-------------------- yr

   (d) English----------------- yrs

6. **Do you like singing songs?**

   (a) Yes (b) No

7. **Can you sing in your own language?**

   (a) Yes (b) No

8. **What are the occasions in which the people of your community sing songs?**

1.______ 2.________ _ 3. ______

4.____________ 5.________ 6. ______

7.________ 8.______ 9.________

10.________

9. **Do you use riddles?**

   (a) Yes (b) No

10. **How often do you use riddles in your conversation?**

    (a) Frequently (b) sometimes (c) occasionally (d) rarely

    (e) never

General Poetry

Q 1. What subjects do you study?

The options provided are:

Prose

Poetry

Non-detail

Writing and Grammar

All of the above

Q 2. Which of them do you think easy and interesting for you?

Prose

Poetry

Non-detail

Writing and Grammar

All of the above

Q 3. Which is difficult and Uninteresting?

Prose

Poetry

Non-detail

Writing and Grammar

All of the above

Q 4. Which subject do you prefer?

Prose Poetry

Q 5. Do you remember any poem that you were taught in High school?

a) Yes (b) No

Q 6. Do you remember it's name?

(a) Yes (b) No

Name of the poem ____________________

Q 7. Rate the poems you are taught

a) Stopping by Woods on a Snowy Evening

1. Difficult

2.Easy
3.Old
4.Boring
5.Interesting

b) Oft, In the Stilly Night
1. Difficult
2.Easy
3.Old
4.Boring
5.Interesting

c) The Inchcape Rock
1. Difficult
2.Easy
3.Old
4.Boring
5.Interesting

d) To My True Friend
1. Difficult
2.Easy
3.Old
4.Boring
5.Interesting

e) Fishing
1. Difficult
2.Easy
3.Old
4.Boring
5.Interesting

Q 8. If difficult, why do you think difficult?

a) Words difficult b) Theme is difficult c) Very long

Q 9. If easy, why do you think easy?

a) Simple language b) Interesting theme c) Short poem

Q 10. From the poems prescribed for you, how much can you understand on your own without the teachers' help?

a) Only 5% b) 10% to 20% c) 30% to 40% d) 50% to 70%

Teaching Poetry

Q1. What steps does your teacher take to teach you a poem?

Does s/he introduce the poem in an interesting way?

Does s/he read aloud the poem?

Does s/he ask you to read the poem silently for some time?

Does s/he ask you questions from the poem?

Does s/he give you interesting task/ activities from the poem?

Does s/he ask you to do these activities in pair/ group?

Q 2. Does s/he explain to you through giving a lecture on the poem and explaining the meaning of the difficult words? (Yes/No)

Q 3. While teaching, does s/he move around the class or just stays near the board and explain/ lecture? (Yes/No)

Q 4. Does s/he use the blackboard? If yes, to what purpose?

Q 5. Who do you consider a good poetry teacher?

One who allows you to understand the poem on your own with little help when necessary

Or

b) One who explains the poem through lectures without allowing you to understand on your own.

Q 6. Does your teacher give you some writing tasks on poems and provide you with feedback? (Yes/No)

Q 7. Does s/he points out your errors and provide you suggestions to improve your English? (Yes/No)

Q 8. What are the questions on tests should be?

a) Short type **b. Long type**

Q 9. How do you prepare for the exam?

Q 10. Do you feel tensed before examination? (Yes/No)

Q 11. What would you like?

Poetry should be removed from your syllabus?

It should stay but poems which are simple and interesting be included which you can understand on your own with little help from the teacher

(Signature Of Student)

Appendix B
Teachers' Questionnaire

Dear Teachers

It is my sincere request to you to fill this questionnaire so that I may get the data much needed for my study. The information collected will be used for research purpose only. I hope, your response will be of immense help in my study.

Thank you.

Preetinanda Roy

Questionnaire for Teachers

Personal Data

1. Name: 2. Qualification:

Teaching Experience:

Total Teaching Experience: Experience of Teaching In KISS:

1. Do you belong to Schedule Tribe?

   (Yes / No)

2. **Are you aware of tribal culture?**

   (Yes / No)

3. **Have you got any special training in teaching English? (If yes, mention the kind of training you have got)?**

   (Yes / No)

4. **Have you got any special training in teaching to tribal learners? (If yes, mention the kind of training you have got)?**

   (Yes / No)

5. **Do you know any tribal languages? (if yes, mention the languages)?**

   (Yes / No)

6. **How is teaching to non-tribal students different from teaching to tribal learners?**

   ____

   ____

   ______

7. **What according to you is most suitable for teaching to the tribal learners?**

   a) Prose b) Poetry c) Non-detail d) Grammar (e) All

8. **Why do you think so?**

   ____

   ____

   ____

9. **Which form of literature is closely related to tribal life and culture?**

   a) Prose b) Poetry c) Non-detail d) Grammar (e) All

10. **In which language do you communicate with your students in the class?**

    (a) English (b) Odia (c) Tribal language (d) specify, if other____________

11. **In which language do you communicate with your students outside the class?**

    (a) English (b) Odia (c) Tribal language (d) specify, if other____________

12. **Here are some opinions expressed by people about the tribals. How many of them do you consider to be true?**

    They are ignorant.

    Their culture is inferior.

    They drink too much.

    They are orthodox and superstitious.

    They are incapable of mental work.

    It is difficult to persuade them.

    They are less intelligent.

    They are difficult to educate.

    They have no idea of cleanliness.

    They are lazy and docile.

    They are quite satisfied with what they have and do not try to improve their lot.

    They are impulsive, short-tempered and emotional.

    They are cruel and fond of physical violence.

    They are cheated easily.

    They are loose in their moral habits.

    They lack courtesy.

13. **What is your opinion in general about the scholastic ability of the tribal students?**

    a) Most of them do well in their studies as the non-tribal students.

    b) They are superior to non-tribal students in studies.

    c) They are inferior to the non-tribal students.

14. **Do you think they have any special educational problems which the non-tribal students don't have?**

(Yes / No)

15. **If your answer to the Q No 14 is Yes, what, in your opinion, are the special difficulties that the tribal students have?**

    a) Their cultural background comes in the way of their receiving modern education.

    b) The poverty of the tribal students is more acute than that of non-tribal students.

    c) Tribal students don't receive enough encouragement from the society.

    d) Their language problems come in their way of education.

    e) They are inherently lazy and not interested in study.

16. **Do you feel that your students have special problems in learning English as compared to non-tribal students?**

    Yes / No / Not Certain

17. **If your answer to question No 16 is yes, what are some of the special problems that tribal students have in learning English?**

    a) The fact that English is third or fourth language for them, where as it is a 2nd or 3rd language for non-tribal students with Odia mother tongue.

    b) The fact that most of the tribal students are first generation learners.

    c) They have special cultural difficulties.

    d) They are poor at learning language in general.

    e) They have less motivation in learning English than non-tribals.

    f) They have no desire to learn English as they think this will lead to a loss of identity.

    g) They have less encouragement from their parents and guardians for learning English than the non-tribal students.

h) They have no idea of the importance of English in the modern world.

18. **Do you think some of the themes and ideas found in the English text books create cultural problems for tribal students?**

    Yes / No

19. **Have you ever felt difficulty in communicating such themes and ideas to them?**

    Never / Rarely / Often

20. Do you think that knowing their culture and language will be an advantage to you in teaching them English?

    Yes / No

General Poetry

1. What subjects do you teach?

   Prose

   Poetry

   Non-detail

   Writing and Grammar

   All of the above

2. **Which of them do you think easy and interesting for you to teach?**

   Prose (b) Poetry (c) Non-detail (d) Grammar and Writing

3. **Which are difficult and uninteresting to teach?**

   a) Prose (b) Poetry (c) Non-detail (d) Grammar and writing

4. **What is the difference between a prose piece and a poem?**

5. **How is teaching of poetry different from teaching of prose?**

6. **What according to you are the objectives of teaching poems?**

7. **Which subject do you prefer to teach personally?**

(a) Prose (b) Poetry

8. What methods of teaching, according to you, are best suited for tribal learners?

(a) Direct method (b) Grammar-translation Method (C) Structural Method

(d) Other Four out of seven teachers said that Grammar-translation method is

9. Why do you think so?

10. Rate the poems that you have taught

a) Stopping by Woods on a Snowy Evening
1. Difficult 2.Easy 3.Old 4.Boring 5.Interesting
b) Oft, In the Stilly Night
1. Difficult 2.Easy 3.Old 4.Boring 5.Interesting
c) The Inchcape Rock
1. Difficult 2.Easy 3.Old 4.Boring 5.Interesting

d) To My True Friend
1. Difficult 2.Easy 3.Old 4.Boring 5.Interesting
e) Fishing
1. Difficult 2.Easy 3.Old 4.Boring 5.Interesting

8. **If difficult, why do you think difficult?**

   (a). Words difficult (b). Theme is difficult (c). Very long

9. **If easy, why do you think easy?**

   (a). Simple language (b). Interesting theme (c). Short poem

10. **From the poems taught by you, how much do you think the learners understand on their own without your help?**

    (a). Only 5% (b). 10% to 20% (c). 30% to 40% (d). 50% to 70%

11. **Do you feel there are a good number of students in your class whose English language is much below their level? If yes, what is their rough percentage in the class?**

    (Yes / No)

12. **What are the probable reasons, according to you, for their weak performance in English?**

Given below are some of the probable reasons, stated by the teachers which are the main cause of weak performance of the tribal students.

Lack of vocabulary

Lack of knowledge on tense, aspect and time

Lack of proficiency in writing

Fear for English

Different cultural background

Difference in mother tongue

Socio-economic background

Lack of creativity

English as third or fourth language

Less cared for in primary classes

De-motivation to learn English

13. **How do you judge that the students have understood the poem after your teaching in the class?**

____

____

____

14. **Which is better to teach language to tribal learners?**

(a). Prose (b). Poetry

15. **Whether poetry should be removed from their syllabus? Why?(Yes/No)**

____

____

____

Teaching Poetry

1. What steps do you take to teach the poem?

introduce the poem in an interesting way

read aloud the poem

ask them to read the poem silently for some time

ask them questions from the poem

give them interesting tasks/ activities from the poem

ask them to do the activities in pair/ group?

2. **Do you explain through giving a lecture on the poem and explaining the meaning of the difficult words?**

(Yes / No)

3. **While teaching do you move around the class or just stay near the board and explain/ lecture?**

   (a). move around the class (b) just stay near the board and explain/ lecture

4. **Do you use the blackboard? If yes, to what purpose?**

   ____

   ____

   ____

5. **What according to you are the traits that a good teacher must possess?**

   One who teaches in simple and interesting ways and allows students to understand it on their own with little help when necessary

   or

   One who selects difficult poems and only explains the poem through lectures without allowing the students to understand on their own.

6. **Do you give some writing tasks on poems and provide them with feedback?**

   (Yes / No)

7. **Do you point out their errors and provide them suggestions to improve their English?**

   (Yes / No)

8. **Have you ever tried to explain the poems using your own methodology and questions other than what has been provided in the text?**

   (Yes / No)

9. **What modifications would you suggest in the present poetry syllabus to make it suitable for tribal learners?**

   Poems should be short and simple

It should be based on tribal culture and theme

There should be more learner centered interesting activities in the syllabus

10. **Do you think the poems taught to them are difficult for those low-proficient learners? If yes, how do you help them?**

Yes, they are difficult. But repeated discussions help.

Yes. I help them by giving them other poems which suit their level.

Yes, explain them in the class, give notes, respond to their questions during or after lectures.

By interpreting the lines at the immediate constituent level/ word level

Yes. Take pains to explain the poems in the simplest possible language which are within their level of comprehension.

Make them read the stanzas many times. Ask them lead questions so that they are led to understand the content.

Not difficult.

11. **What are the suggestions for helping them to learn in your poetry class?**

Select poems which suit their level; Select poems which can profitably be used to teach them English language; Design learner-friendly tasks from the poem

Reading aloud the poem in group, doing activities

Make them read and enjoy poetry free from conditions imposed by examination; ask them right questions to simulate interest in various aspects of poetry

By group activities, they should make friendship with like-minded persons and 'each one teach one' principle should be followed by them. I will supervise their activities.

Force them to participate in the process of learning by promoting activities. Teacher talks less and students do more activities.

Selection of good poems is of crucial importance. Then motivating the students to understand the beauty and value of the experience contained in the poems is also very important.

Motivation and repeated reading

Suggest for reading more

12. **Should they be taught in their own language?**

    (Yes / No)

13. **While teaching, do you stick to teacher's place or move around the class?**

    Both-more moving around

    move around

    stick to teacher's place

    as per the situation in the class

    all the time move around to promote involvement in the activities sometimes I do move around the class if the class is not very large and if the classroom is not very congested

14. **Given below are some ways of teaching poems. Tick as many as you agree?**

    Introduce the poem

    Provide pre-reading activities

    Read aloud the poem

    Read aloud and then explain

    Allow students to read silently

    Ask questions to the students from the poem

    While asking, advise the students to close the handouts/ books

Provide tasks/ activities on the poem

15. **How do you test the students? Tick as many as you really do.**

Set long answer type questions

Set short answer type questions

Both a & b

Set explanations from the poems taught

Provide a poem not in the course and ask comprehension questions from the poem

Provide feedback to the students on their performance

16. **Do you think your students enjoy poems in English?**

Yes, provided poems are not old and difficult. – but suits their level and are interesting for them (not for me)

Yes

Yes, they always do

This question is irrelevant to me. Students should be asked this question. But I hope they do enjoy, their feedback proves it.

No doubt about it

Yes, they do. As I stated above, much depends on the selection of the poems by the teacher and then drawing the attention of the students to the beauty and value of the poetic experience which, though subjective in a sense, is of universal nature.

Definitely, yes.

(Signature of Teacher)

Kalinga Institute of Social Sciences

Test Script

Time-1hr Marks-25

Q. 1. Answer the following questions in 4/5 sentences. 4x5

What do you mean by "Miles to go before I sleep"?

What does "other days" mean?

How does the poet recall his friends?

"He will not see me stopping here". What does this expression mean?

Describe the "catch".

Q. 2. Answer the following questions in one sentence. 2x9

Where does the owner of the woods live?

Where did the poet run?

What did he throw with a fervent wish?

Where was his eye on?

What was steady in the ocean?

What are now broken?

What does he give a shake?

What did his friend understand of the poet?

Who was ringing his knell?

Q 3. Complete the sentences. 1x12

a) My little .... must .... it queer

To .... without a farm .... near

Between the .... And the frozen ....

The .... evening of the year.

(think, stop, horse, woods, house, lake, darkest)

b) I thought .... I'd return home

And would .... the jeers of some

I .... My line with a fervent ....

"Oh God, today please give me a ....

(Threw, Fish, fishless, face)

------All the Best-----

Index